Coordinating history across the primary school

THE SUBJECT LEADER'S HANDBOOKS

Series Editor: Mike Harrison, Centre for Primary Education,
School of Education, The University of Manchester,
Oxford Road, Manchester, M13 9DP

Coordinating mathematics across the primary school
Tony Brown

Coordinating English at Key Stage 1
Mick Waters and Tony Martin

Coordinating English at Key Stage 2
Mick Waters and Tony Martin

Coordinating science across the primary school
Lynn D. Newton and Douglas P. Newton

Coordinating information and communications technology across the
primary school
Mike Harrison

Coordinating art across the primary school
Judith Piotrowski, Robert Clements and Ivy Roberts

Coordinating design and technology across the primary school
Alan Cross

Coordinating geography across the primary school
John Halocha

Coordinating history across the primary school
Julie Davies and Jason Redmond

Coordinating music across the primary school
Sarah Hennessy

Coordinating religious education across the primary school
Derek Bastide

Coordinating physical education across the primary school
Carole Raymond

Management skills for SEN coordinators
Sylvia Phillips, Jennifer Goodwin and Rosita Heron

Building a whole school assessment policy
Mike Wintle and Mike Harrison

The curriculum coordinator and the OFSTED inspection
Phil Gadsby and Mike Harrison

Coordinating the curriculum in the smaller primary school
Mick Waters

Coordinating history across the primary school

Julie Davies and Jason Redmond

FALMER PRESS
Taylor & Francis Group

UK	The Falmer Press, 1 Gunpowder Square, London, EC4A 3DE
USA	The Falmer Press, Taylor & Francis Inc., 1900 Frost Road, Suite 101, Bristol, PA 19007

First published in 1998

A catalogue record for this book is available from the British Library

ISBN 0 7507 0691 0 paper

Library of Congress Cataloging-in-Publication Data are available on request

Jacket design by Carla Turchini

Typeset in 10/14pt Melior and printed by Graphicraft Typesetters Ltd., Hong Kong

Contents

Part one
The role of the history coordinator

Part two
What history coordinators need to know

Part three
Whole school policies and schemes of work

Part four
Monitoring for Quality

Part five
Resources for learning

Series editor's preface

This book has been prepared for primary teachers charged with the responsibility of acting as the history coordinator for their school. It forms part of a series of new publications that set out to advise such teachers on the complex issues of improving teaching and learning through managing each element of the primary school curriculum.

Why is there a need for such a series? Most authorities recognise, after all, that the quality of primary children's work and learning depends upon the skills of their class teacher, not in the structure of management systems, policy documents or the titles and job descriptions of staff. Many today recognise that school improvement equates directly to the improvement of teaching so surely all tasks, other than imparting subject knowledge, are merely a distraction for the committed primary teacher.

Nothing should take teachers away from their most important role, that is, serving the best interests of the class of children in their care and this book and the others in the series do not wish to diminish that mission. However, the increasing complexity of the primary curriculum and society's expanding expectations, makes it very difficult for the class teacher to keep up to date with every development. Within traditional subject areas there has been an explosion of knowledge and new fields introduced such as science, technology, design, problem solving and health education, not to mention the uses of computers. These are now considered entitlements for primary children. Furthermore, we now expect all children to succeed at these studies, not just the fortunate few. All this has overwhelmed a class teacher system largely unchanged since the inception of primary schools.

Primary class teachers cannot possibly be experts in every aspect of the curriculum they are required to teach. To whom can they turn for help? It is unrealistic to assume that such support will be available from the headteacher whose responsibilities have grown ever wider since the 1988 Educational Reform Act. Constraints, including additional staff costs, and the loss of benefits from the strength and security of the class teacher system, militate against wholesale adoption of specialist or semi-specialist teaching. Help therefore has to come from exploiting the talents of teachers themselves, in a process of mutual support. Hence primary schools have chosen many and varied systems of consultancy or subject coordination which best suit the needs of their children and the current expertise of the staff.

In fact, curriculum leadership functions in primary schools have increasingly been shared with class teachers through the policy of curriculum coordination for the past twenty years, especially to improve the consistency of work in language and mathematics. Since then each school has developed their own system and the series recognises that the system each reader is part of will be a compromise between the ideal and the possible. Campbell and Neill (1994) show that by 1991 nearly nine out of every ten primary class teachers had such responsibility and the average number of subjects each was between 1.5 and 2.2 (depending on the size of school).

These are the people for whom this series sets out to help to do this part of their work. The books each deal with specific issues whilst at the same time providing an overview of general themes in the management of the subject curriculum. The term *subject leader* is used in an inclusive sense and combines the two major roles that such teachers play when they have responsibility for subjects and aspects of the primary curriculum.

The books each deal with:

- coordination — a role which emphasises; harmonising, bringing together, making links, establishing routines and common practice; and
- subject leadership — a role which emphasises providing information, offering expertise and direction, guiding the development of the subject, and raising standards.

The purpose of the series is to give practical guidance and support to teachers; in particular what to do and how to do it. They each offer help on the production, development and review of policies and schemes of work; the organisation of resources; and developing strategies for improving the management of the subject curriculum.

Each book in the series contains material that subject managers will welcome and find useful in developing their subject expertise and in tackling problems of enthusing and motivating staff.

Each book has five parts.

1 The review and development of the different roles coordinators are asked to play.
2 Updating subject knowledge and subject pedagogical knowledge.
3 Developing and maintaining policies and schemes of work.
4 Monitoring work within the school to enhance the continuity of teaching and progression in pupils' learning.
5 Resources and contacts.

Although written primarily for teachers who are history coordinators, Julie Davies' and Jason Redmond's book offers practical guidance and many insights for anyone in the school who has a responsibility for the history curriculum, including teachers with an overall role in coordinating the whole or key stage curriculum and the deputy head and headteacher.

The book's authors offer many practical hints and useful advice in order that coordinators can establish and maintain history as an important and interesting part of the school's curriculum. It will help those attempting to develop a whole-school view of the progress children make in learning history and in the way they learn to be historians. Julie draws on her considerable experience as a teacher educator, including a period as editor of *Primary Historian* and Jason, a history graduate and recent entrant to the profession, offers an insight as a newly appointed coordinator and primary teacher. Together the authors have put together a most readable book which will help readers develop both the subject expertise they will need and the managerial perspective necessary to enthuse and inform others.

Mike Harrison, Series Editor
January 1998

Introduction

This book sets out to help teachers improve the quality of history teaching and learning as the history subject manager in a primary school. In order to become an effective subject manager, a teacher will need to have specific specialist knowledge of history, an enthusiasm and commitment to its place in the school curriculum and an enduring interest in reviewing practices of teaching in the light of their effectiveness in encouraging learning. The five parts of the book will look at particular aspects of the subject manager's job and provide ideas which will aid the development of the knowledge, skills and concepts needed to carry out the responsibility.

'History is not about facts, it's about evidence'

Part one

The role of the history coordinator

Chapter 1
History and you: getting started

Chapter 2
Developing skills to become an effective history coordinator

| Chapter 1 | History and you: getting started |

On learning that you are to become the subject manager for history, you may feel a sense of pleasurable anticipation at this opportunity. If this is followed by a concern about the weight of the task ahead, and a temporary questioning of your own ability and suitability for leadership, this is a perfectly normal response. What is important is that you understand that everyone has these doubts. The crucial question to ask is — How can I do the best job possible, for the children, the school and my colleagues? This opening chapter is intended to give you support in a practical way, so that you have a temporary survival kit to help you in the early stages as a subject manager.

Know yourself

One of the first things that you must do as a subject manager is to look honestly at yourself in the light of what you believe the job entails and how close you are to matching its requirements. This is an important first step in coming to terms with what you perceive as any discrepancy in what you believe the job entails and your ability to fulfil its requirements.

Think about

- Do you really know enough about the subject?
- Are you aware of how the subject is taught within your school?
- Do you know of any existing subject-related documentation?

It may be that the area of history is well developed within your school and your job will entail fine tuning and monitoring the subject, or it may be that your school is in the process of developing a new policy and scheme of work in the light of the new National Curriculum Orders. At the precise moment that your headteacher asks you if you will take over history, all these thoughts are irrelevant. The only things that matter are:

■ your level of interest and enthusiasm for history as a subject,
■ your view of yourself as an historian,
■ your knowledge of history, both as a subject and in the context of children's development in learning the skills necessary to be historians, and the 'facts' necessary to be historically aware.

This is where you need to be honest with yourself and do a personal audit of what history you know. There is no point imagining that you will be an effective subject manager without an ounce of knowledge about the subject, but neither will anyone expect you to know or learn everything. There would never be enough time to do this and it would be pointless anyway. You cannot teach all the history in the school, so why know it all? What you must have, though, is a basic grounding of knowledge, and enough know-how in the area to be able to offer advice to colleagues, and point them in the right direction. Your job is to facilitate the effective learning of history in your school, by advising and monitoring your colleagues. It is not your job to take the world on your shoulders, metaphorically, and know everything.

This section will concentrate on areas that you personally need to examine, in order to meet your needs as an effective subject manager, and the needs of the school as a result. In the following sections, our aim is to examine both the self development needed by a newly qualified teacher (NQT) taking on their first area of responsibility, and the needs of an experienced teacher, given the role of history subject manager for the first time. The experiences of each make it necessary to look at their needs separately. Some strategies are needed and used by all subject managers, of course, and these will be examined in the following sections.

How much work is going on in history?

As a classroom teacher, based in either Key Stage 1 or 2, it is very possible you have not been into other teachers' rooms or even walked all around the school. Now is the time to do this. Fact-finding, collecting empirically based evidence and making notes are all facets of a historian's skill, these are what you will need to get a first impression of exactly what history is in evidence around the school. A key fact to remember is that all schools teach history. They have to, it is a statutory requirement, and, somewhere in your school, no matter how unlikely it may appear at first, there is history being taught well. Wherever it is happening, it is something that you need to seize on and celebrate. This will show those who are insecure in the subject that it can be done well — within a busy classroom environment with a thousand other things to do. As subject manager, it must be your aim to extend the success, and build on the good practice that already exists. Do not hesitate to praise the teachers in your school who are doing their best despite the obstacles that are in their way. Everyone responds to a little bit of praise and it may have the additional effect of making them somewhat more responsive to other suggestions you may have.

A walk around the school will help you to start to gain a feel for the position of history in the school. Take a notebook with you and jot down the things that you find.

You can start in the corridors and hall. Look at displays around the school — what do they tell you about the status of history? Displays in public areas tend to be developed on a rota system (for example — 'Your turn to do the entrance hall'). They will indicate classroom foci at particular times of the year and, therefore, there should be some history publicly displayed somewhere. If not, you should ask why not.

Look in classrooms — is there any evidence of history on the walls or on display in three dimensional work? History may be taught either as a regular weekly lesson or as a block in the timetable; either way, you would expect at least one classroom to have some evidence on display. If not, why not.

Is there any staffroom chat about the subject? General staff pre-occupations usually become items for staff meetings, so noting anything on the subject of history is an important beginning for putting history on the agenda.

Where does history feature in curriculum planning forecasts? The school development plan will reveal what is to be taught and you can use this information as a marker for offering help to particular teachers at times of their greatest interest in history. By considering such questions you may begin to develop a feel for the task ahead.

Other considerations to be acted upon include:
- Talk to the headteacher to determine his or her attitude.
- Examine school documentation of all kinds. If there has been a recent OFSTED inspection, what were the implications for history? This report could be your ally in your commitment to enhancing the quality of history teaching and learning in your school. If the report is somewhat negative, the action plan developed to improve matters will be the result of staff meetings and will be a focus for the way forward.
- Make sure you have read the latest advice from the School Curriculum and Assessment Authority (SCAA) as well as the most recent subject guidelines for OFSTED inspectors as set out in the handbook.

In order to broaden your own experience of history and to begin to join a network of people outside school, make contact with a local adviser, or school, college or university where advice may be available. If you are an NQT it may be worth returning to a school where you have completed a teaching practice and talking to the history manager. You will almost always be given advice willingly by someone you have worked with as a student teacher. In addition, take note of any courses which might help you or your colleagues. Enquire about any national association for teachers of your subject. Do they have a primary section? Do they have local meetings?

You will have to strengthen the links with the local community in order to fulfil the National Curriculum requirements.
- How has the local study unit been planned?
- Does the local community fit in?

One of the teachers will have to plan the compulsory local study unit. What help can the local residents be here? You need to access oral history as part of the children's history entitlement at both Key Stages among the families, the shopkeepers, local tradespeople of all sorts, as well as among the professions which service the community. Have your colleagues looked at the local community with this in mind? They may be unaware of the wealth of material for this aspect of history that exists on their doorstep.

Keep a record

As a historian, you know how important written evidence is and, therefore, as a subject manager, you will find keeping a portfolio of your activity helpful. It will help you to show development and progress over time in your role and to demonstrate your success. The file should contain your notes, relevant documents and your diary and you will be able to use it when you talk to the headteacher as it will help establish a professional dialogue. Through reference to your notes, talk about the current priority history has, in your view, within the school development plan. Emphasise your interest in and commitment to the place of history in children's work. Discuss your priorities and formulate a rationale and targets for your work — especially with regard to any formal documentation, such as the need to develop or revise the school history policy. After this initial meeting, start to think in terms of a plan of action at the classroom level.

Arrange to visit other teachers' classrooms

You will need to consider the reasons you give teachers for your presence — whether you are an NQT or have had twenty years' teaching experience.

Think about the best way to get into teachers' rooms without making them feel uncomfortable or insecure in their teaching ability. Often the teacher in the next classroom to you will be used to you popping in and out to share resources so that may be the best place to start. If you do manage to get into a classroom, what will you do with the information that you gather? Is this information for the headteacher, deputy, the governors, senior management team or for the class teacher only? Is this decision yours to make? Remember, traditionally primary teachers do not observe the lessons of their colleagues and do not offer comment on colleagues' teaching styles,

Think about

Are you there:
■ as a critical friend to focus on an area the teacher has identified?
■ to discover the quality of the work in history in that classroom?
■ to give you an idea of progression in children's skills across the school?

approach and lesson plans, or act as critical friends. For this reason, subject managers have often proved reluctant to direct colleagues or suggest ideas. Recently, with peer review of teaching developing, teachers have had to come to terms with the idea of being watched and their performance evaluated and discussed with them.

In order for the role of subject manager to evolve from simply writing policies and offering tips, there needs to be a genuine whole school commitment to improving standards of teaching performance. This may then result in a more open door approach on the part of teachers towards subject coordinators. While you are working towards this state of affairs, you may be able to create a climate of change by inviting colleagues into your room to see some aspect of history that you feel needs to be improved upon, or incorporated within colleagues' history teaching. Other ways of beginning the process of change might include:

■ inviting a speaker into school;
■ displaying articles or reviews;
■ running a workshop;
■ asking a colleague to trial a new approach or recently published material;
■ reporting back to colleagues on a course you have attended.

If you are managing history for the first time in your school, the first thing that you need to do is see history taught in your school by other members of staff. It is important that you gain experience from your colleagues, but as a subject manager, it will also be invaluable for you to see how different teachers approach the subject. In one school recently, we witnessed approaches as varied as a 'hands-on' session involving artefacts borrowed from a local authority to a concentrated comprehension session using text books. No doubt, you will find similar lessons in your school.

An important feature of the history teaching in your school is to consider to what extent does it change throughout the school? For example, when watching Key Stage 1 history, you can be made aware of how easy it is for those teachers to fall into the trap of relying too heavily on one aspect of history, the story telling, without really breaking into the use of source material. In Key Stage 2, you may see that the reverse is true — too little story and too many sources.

How children's recording of their history learning develops throughout their six years is a feature you must keep up-to-date on. The easiest and, probably most informative, way to do this, is to look at children's exercise books. With this aim in mind, it is worth borrowing books from various classes to examine the various teaching approaches to written history. Teachers with responsibility for history, working in a school which has more than one form entry should also keep close watch on the books of classes in the same year. Generally, you need to become aware of the history that goes on around you, and the different approaches that different teachers have. A little personal knowledge of how your colleagues teach the subject will certainly be useful when drawing up a realistic, workable policy document, and absolutely crucial when designing a scheme of work.

A more experienced member of staff would perhaps not need to carry out this area of self development to the extent that an NQT should. As an experienced member of staff, you will have taught history before, perhaps through different year groups, and key stages, and you should have a fair knowledge of the different approaches to history that go on in your school, simply through the everyday conversations in the staffroom. However, it may be worth your while to see a whole history lesson in a year group in which you have no experience, and it would certainly be worthwhile to borrow a few of the children's books from different year groups to see exactly what your colleagues are covering.

Sources of information about history in your school
Areas to examine when auditing history:
- your own knowledge of history, and of the National Curriculum for history;
- curriculum planning documents — long, medium or short term planning;
- displays in public areas, e.g. halls, corridors;
- classroom displays;
- children's books;
- any recent documents/reports regarding history in your school;
- your colleagues.

Initial notes on these items could be used to begin to develop your subject manager's portfolio.

Request a budget to support your work

This allocation will enable you to buy and use resources without continual recourse to your headteacher. Your argument for this money will be strengthened if the school development plan indicates history should be a focus for development or if you have done an audit which indicates severe weaknesses in any area. Once you have the money, arrange to find a method of gaining agreement amongst the staff for its use.

Set out the options and their costs and get a discussion going about what to prioritise. There may be a conflict of needs — for example, Key Stage 1 has insufficient artefacts while Years 3 and 6 have no written sources for their units on the Ancient Greeks and Tudors. Setting out the needs of individual groups of children in this way will allow the whole staff to discuss the problems and find some solution. Compromise solutions, where money is allocated across identified needs so that everyone gets something is one way. Another solution might be to sort one area of need out properly (Key Stage 1 artefacts) and timetable the others for the next budget round.

Record the results of any meetings (formal or informal) you have had to determine spending of this fund and include this record with an end of year account of how the money was spent. Hand this in to the headteacher even if he or she has not asked for it. You will show by this action that you accept that accountability is a necessary corollary to responsibility.

Become aware of the ways in which children learn history

Perhaps the only way of doing this is by structuring a historical activity that can be adapted for different year groups, and then doing it! This will require the cooperation of your colleagues and will involve either working in their classes or taking groups of children out to do the activity. Explain to them that what you will find out about how children learn history will be invaluable when you come to start your official documentation such as the policy, because you will be aware of the differing needs of your colleagues according to the age group they are teaching. Perhaps even more importantly, it will provide you with an insight that will help you when you come to offer advice to your colleagues. As an NQT with limited experience of Key Stage 2, for example, you may find it difficult to understand the needs of these older children, and so your advice would become less useful than it should be. The activity we have detailed below has been tried in school with Year 1, Year 3 and Year 6 children, and will, in itself, provide you with considerable insight into the way that children learn history.

The task involves the story of Dick Whittington, which is a well known story that most children will have heard at some point in their lives.

The task should contain the following major elements:
- there should be a discussion of the time the story is set in and the chronology of the events within it;
- there should be an attempt to discuss continuity and change, with the similarities and differences between our time and Dick Whittington's examined;
- discuss whether the story is true or not, and how we could find out. (It may be possible to present Year 6 children with two different versions of the story, and discuss why the stories are different, and which one they think is true).

How you might proceed:

1 When asking children to retell the story, ask Year One children to draw a small number of pictures (four, perhaps), and ask the older children to write it down in a certain number of sentences, limiting the number for the older children.
2 Use illustrations in a story book to ask about the differences that are apparent between then and now. Also, include a search for similarities, often ignored but just as important. For example, modes of transport, clothing, houses, street furniture etc.
3 A tape recorder may be useful for taping the answers to your questions regarding the story's place in history, and will be invaluable in recording replies concerning the 'truth' or otherwise of the story.

What you should find is a progression of historical skill development throughout the age ranges. You may find that Year 1 children will have a fairly solid grasp of events that are similar to their own, and will be able to compare pictures in a book to their own experiences. However, when you go beyond their experience, you may be surprised at the lack of historical reasoning (after all, we take it for granted). Two examples we have come across include the Year 1 child who told us confidently that the story took place last March (!), and the numerous times that we have been told that the story cannot be true because it happened before the children's parents were born! By Year 6, you should be able to see a significant difference in the children's historical skill and knowledge. They should be able to place the story somewhere near its fifteenth century origins (many will say it took place during the time of the Tudors), and perhaps more importantly, they will be able to see beyond their own personal experiences, and offer plausible reasons for events and opinions based on a more general knowledge.

The exercise is a more than worthwhile activity, because it will provide you with first hand knowledge of the sort of progression that is demanded by the National Curriculum, and that will have to be catered for in your history policies and schemes of work for the school. You cannot hope to frame a document which aims for a progression in the Key Elements without having some awareness of what that progression looks like, sounds like and acts like, and how that progression can be incorporated into your colleagues' history work in realistic ways. That you have used actual children from actual classes in your school means you can refer to individuals and their responses when you talk to the staff. This will give credibility to what you are trying to do and will interest the teachers because it is centred on their children.

Develop a superficial knowledge of the areas to be studied

The first rule for this acquisition of knowledge is — don't overstretch yourself. There is little enough time to teach as it is, and trying to learn the history of Britain to degree standard will not help. You need to be realistic. Again, let us look at the two different starting points we have given. For an experienced teacher, the job will not be as difficult, there should be a basic knowledge of at least a couple of the study units, through your current teaching, although you may feel the need to refresh areas you have not taught for a while.

As an NQT, it may be that you will need to start from scratch, but there is a manageable way to do this. The easiest, quickest and most profitable way to learn a superficial amount of knowledge for each study unit is to read some of the books that teachers in your school would give to the children. Be wary of taking them at face value, as some of the textbooks on offer are far from excellent, and sometimes far from accurate. This is why you will need to read at least three books on each unit, to ensure that you receive at least some balance in the things that you learn. This really does not take very long at all. We have known it done in a fortnight during term time. This background reading provides you with two things; first a superficial knowledge of each study unit or each event or famous person covered at your school; second, you are road testing the school's book-based history resources. After you have finished your reading, it is likely that you will have read each of the text books from each Key Stage 2 study unit that your school possesses. From this direct knowledge it will be possible for you to evaluate, at a later date, the resource needs of the subject. If you read a text book and feel that it provided you with little or no worthwhile information, why should the children feel any different? If a text book was excellent and informative, does the same company produce any other books that may be of use? Make a note of your reaction to the books for future reference.

By building on your now superficial, broad knowledge of the content required by the National Curriculum you will find that you are more able to offer colleagues advice on the subject, or at least tell them where they can find things out if they need to. It will also be worth your while to try and spot gaps in the books you read. A good example of this is the complete absence of any women in one text book on the Anglo-Saxons, and amazingly, the even more unbelievable absence of any black people in a text book about the Ancient Egyptians. These are serious flaws, and would need to be rectified.

Assess the resources

This leads on to the next area of developing your own knowledge so that you can become an effective manager of the subject. You need to be aware of what resources you have in school for the high quality teaching and learning experiences that the National Curriculum demands in the subject. Absences from text books are one thing of which you need to be very aware. It would be impossible to teach 'Everyday Life', a stipulation in all of the study units, without teaching about the roles of women, for example. It may be difficult for you to find the information you need to ensure that all races, sexes and cultures are studied within your school's history teaching, but it is something that you must do. Check the school's history resources with this need for sexual, racial and cultural equality in mind and check the content of the books against the requirements of the study units that they should be covering. Are all the areas covered? Which areas are not mentioned, and do separate resources exist for these? Also, check the Key Elements resources with the resources provided by your school. Within the teaching of history in Key Stages 1 and 2, it is a statutory requirement that children's enquiries include studying the following:

pictures and photographs;
written accounts including documents and printed sources;
artefacts;
music;
buildings and sites.

Key Stage 1 Key Elements also includes mention, although non-statutory, of films and television programmes, plays and museum displays.

Does your school possess all of these items or have access to them? Are there any shortfalls, even in single study units? For example, one school we are aware of is extremely well resourced for Ancient Greece, including numerous pieces of replica pottery, but has no artefacts at all for its study of the Aztecs. This is a significant shortfall, and one that a history subject manager should be aware of, and seek to rectify.

You will only know if shortfalls exist if you speak to your colleagues about the history they have taught and the resources they claim to need. It may be that they wished to expand on one particular area of study within a unit, but were unable to do so because of a lack of resources in that specific area — something that a simple audit may miss.

Understand teachers' and children's views of history

Perhaps the key to self development is a willingness to learn from other teachers, regardless of whether you have no experience at all, or have taught for twenty years. There is always more to learn, and always something of which you were unaware. You need to approach colleagues, and speak to them about history, how they teach it and what they teach. Speak to children, and find out what they think of history. You will be amazed how much a five minute chat with a child from another class can yield. Most importantly, you must be honest with yourself. If there are shortcomings in your knowledge then try to remedy them. If you feel that you lack experience of a particular age group, then observe them learning. Try to find out as much as you can about how children's historical ability develops, as this will be of great benefit to you when you come to work with colleagues on the writing of documents such as schemes of work and policies. Before you can help your colleagues with their history teaching, you must help yourself. In this way, the advice that you offer will be grounded in reality, not fantasy, and will assist you colleagues in ensuring that their history teaching is of high quality, where children's learning can progress positively.

This first reaction to being given the history subject manager's brief should settle your immediate and most pressing concerns. It is now time to take a more measured and reflective look at this job and what it will entail.

Chapter 2

Developing skills to become an effective history coordinator

You have the opportunity, through your effective management of history to improve teachers' teaching and children's learning in your school. This chapter sets out the many things you have to think about if this opportunity is to become a reality. We have used the writings of Harrison (1995, a and b) as the basis for this chapter.

You know that the challenge of working with colleagues to produce an effective programme in any subject area is one which will contribute to personal development and enhance the image of the profession. What you have to impart to the staff is the fact that you subscribe to the truism that the key to quality in primary education lies in the skills of the class teacher. Indeed, that at the heart of the educational process lies the teacher, for, at its best, education concerns itself with the whole child, provides for secure relationships and covers all aspects of a child's development. For the teachers to know how highly you rate their significance to children's learning is an added help when you seek to persuade them to try out new techniques or materials in their history teaching. If they see that you appreciate the complexity of the curriculum and society's high expectations of them, they will be more likely to listen and respond or ask you for advice. You, in turn, must expect that a range of responsibilities will be devolved upon you, some of which you can effectively manage while some you may not be able to deal with in a way you would like. The reason for the latter state of affairs will rest in the history, personalities and ethos of the school in which you work. These pressures will be different in different schools, but all subject managers will have to face them to some extent. It may be useful, then, to look at the factors within schools which impinge on the subject manager's job.

It is a truism that a successful team needs people with specific skills, knowledge, aptitudes, interests and personalities which interlock in order to make a workable organization. You will have to work with the understanding that your team may or may not have such ideally interlocking personalities. You must also appreciate that the headteacher also has to suffer the same mix of personalities, probably inheriting staff they themselves would not have chosen. Those appointed ten years ago were selected to fit the situation at the time. Now new skills and attitudes are needed, but not everyone can change so easily. Thus you must work within the constraints of the nature of your teacher colleagues. The only way forward is to work with them and appreciate that however enthusiastic you are about your proposals, subject management, like politics (perhaps even more so), is the art of the possible. You must recognise that teams need leaders and the head is the leader of the school. As such, and also because the head has chosen you to do a particular job of some importance, he or she deserves your support and help. If this is given by you then you might expect the same in return.

The time needed to become a proficient subject manager is an important consideration. It is important that your views on this are rehearsed with the head and staff (who will all be subject managers probably, and consequently have a vested interest in this issue). You will tactfully remind everyone that the time made available for subject managers to do the paperwork will affect the degree of consultation possible and hence its quality. Similarly, time for subject managers to work alongside their colleagues in their classrooms will be necessary in order to change practice. You may need time to see teaching and learning in parts of the school with which you are unfamiliar in order to develop your professional skills. You may find headteachers agreeing with these sentiments as well as your colleagues. However, if you are still not provided with non-contact time you will find it difficult to do some of the things

The nature of the decisions subject managers feel confident in making without recourse to the headteacher;

the mechanisms by which the work of the subject managers is monitored;

the choice of particular teachers to be subject managers and the way they are managed;

the strength of the systems in place to support subject management (e.g. class release time, training);

whether subject managers are respected as models of good practice in their specialist areas;

the ways in which subject managers are encouraged to learn personnel management skills from one another;

the degree to which subject managers are able to work in harmony with the school's stated aims.

mentioned. You can come to a decision about how much personal time you are willing to devote to this role, bearing in mind your classteacher's workload and the need for rest and recreation. One way forward towards getting non-contact time would be to emphasise that the role of subject manager implies managerial skill as well as curricular expertise, thus teachers selected to become subject managers would need to develop skills in areas such as the implementation of change, curriculum planning, evaluation and school development, in addition to attending subject based courses. If this argument were accepted, it would not be possible for a reasonable headteacher to resist the pressure to provide non-contact time for subject managers.

In order to measure how far down the line your school is in developing policies for these things to happen, Harrison and Gill (1992) drew up a checklist of indicators. (It is set out, in the box; as an aid for you to make use of, not as a stick to beat yourself with when you find nothing like it going on in your school):

It would be enlightening for you to consider each of the listed points as they may apply to you in your school. Discuss with the headteacher the validity of these statements as indicators of the strength of an effective subject management system. Does the outcome of the discussion give you a clearer idea of what the headteacher expects of you? Similarly, does reflection on these points help you define the ethos of the school? Use the list to consider the ways colleagues relate to one another and to you. Consider the customs, the leadership styles on display and how you might use this awareness to influence other teachers. The importance of working within these parameters which determine the culture of the school cannot be overemphasised. Whether your influence as a subject manager is for good or ill, its strength will depend on the way you personally approach the task. By considering your actions with care, you can determine the most appropriate way to ensure maximum impact on your colleagues.

Where to start

Cross and Harrison (1994) suggest a strategy for this to begin to happen.

> They suggest that subject managers need to persuade, cajole (if necessary) and affect the attitudes of staff towards:
> - the need for change;
> - the focus of the change (for example, planning a study unit or resources);
> - the change process itself.

Change will not be achieved because you wish it, or through government legislation or incidental INSET. Change only occurs when teachers believe in the need for it, know where it is going, are committed to it and have some ownership of it. So you have a central role in making things happen in the history entitlement of the children.

> The key personal skills which you will need to develop in order to promote curricular change include the ability to:
>
> act consistently;
> maintain hope and optimism;
> want success;
> be willing to take calculated risks and accept the consequences;
> develop a capacity to accept, deal with and use conflict constructively;
> learn to use a soft voice and low key manner;
> develop self-awareness;
> cultivate a tolerance of ambiguity and complexity;
> avoid viewing issues as simply black and white;
> become an active listener (adapted from Everard and Morris, 1985).

Nobody ever said it was going to be easy, but with a determination to improve the teaching of history, and an ability to adapt this determination to different situations, you will find yourself achieving positive changes.

Effective communication strategies

You need to communicate effectively at all levels if you want to make a positive contribution to children's history learning and teachers' history teaching. The skills to bring this about have been itemised several times in various books. The list below is based on the principles in Joan Dean's (1987) book 'Managing the Primary School':

1 teachers are more likely to be responsive to your advice if it
   is addressed personally to them as individuals rather than
   addressed anonymously in a staff meeting or by memo. That
   is, as long as the advice is given in a professional manner,
   with due consideration to the person you are addressing,
   and their attitudes and feelings;

2 arousing the interest of the listener is necessary if you want
   to get your message across. To ensure this, make sure that
   what you are trying to say is interesting and relevant;

3 information is more likely to be valued if it gives an
   advantage in power or status to the listener. For example,
   if you do this, your teaching will become even more
   accomplished;

4 as the status of the source of information is often seen to
   indicate its importance, there may be an advantage in
   choosing an appropriate messenger on occasion, such as
   the headteacher or a senior member of staff;

5 time and place should be chosen carefully in order to
   predispose the listener to be receptive to your ideas. Don't
   be afraid to shelve your ideas for a while. If you approach
   a colleague on a bad day, or they are busy with another
   task, it is better to wait to deliver your ideas when they
   are listening than to have them ignored by a tired, fedup
   teacher desperate to go home.

Getting the most out of meetings

Meetings are the most common method used to get messages
across, yet they are not always successful because the central
issue of outcomes are not kept in the forefront of your mind. To
help you focus on this there follows a set of reasons why you
may need to hold a meeting and what you can do to maximise
your message's impact (based on Harrison, 1995a & b).

Communicate information

As history subject manager you will often need to give
information to colleagues, such as the dates and location of a
local history book exhibition or the list of resources that have
newly arrived in the school. This information is best given out
in written form with only a brief explanation. The skill you will

need to develop is to ensure that the information is read and acted upon. Wasting everyone's time by either not providing a briefing sheet containing the information or spending an hour laboriously going over it in too much detail, is sure to alienate you from your colleagues. Teachers dislike time-wasting in any form. The key is to be brief and arouse interest.

Discuss issues publicly

In order to get the most out of this session you will need to provide the staff with the relevant information beforehand so that they can come to the meeting properly prepared. You will need to create a non-threatening atmosphere for all members of staff to feel confident that their views will be valued even if they cause disagreement. You need to be aware that reception teachers are least likely to offer any views in a staff meeting and you should work as leader of the meeting to include everyone. This will get easier as time goes on and the staff realise that everyone is expected to have a say. It might be useful to use brainstorming techniques sometimes so that the forum for discussion is less formal. You will always need to have as an aim the creation of an atmosphere that is encouraging and open if productive discussion is your aim.

Make decisions together

Everyone who attends a meeting of this nature must be made aware beforehand that that is the purpose for the meeting. It follows that time will have been spent at other meetings discussing the factors surrounding the decision to be made. For example, the need for a new set of textbooks for an area of the history curriculum is recognised by the staff. The choice of which set to go for will be reached only after close inspection of the possible choices and how they will fit into the school's present resource bank. A meeting to come to this important decision will need to be carefully managed by you so that everyone feels they have had their say. This is important for the future effective and widespread use of this purchase.

Before going on to talk about how you can influence the staff through INSET, it might be useful to mention other aspects of the role you need to be working on. You, as subject manager,

---

Suggestion

There is no need to labour the point further that you will be more effective as a subject manager if you appreciate the various purposes of staff meetings and realise how to manage them.

will need to pay close attention to the relationships you develop with:

Relationships with colleagues

The headteacher

The importance of getting on with the leader of the school cannot be overemphasised. Show enthusiasm for your subject area through your classroom work, your attendance at INSET meetings and the way your children approach history.

Other subject managers

There could be rivalry for the limited amount of money available. This will cause dissension unless you can persuade them of the need for a fair distribution of funds over time and based on the school development plan. If subject managers see that their subject has been given due consideration, they are more prepared to wait their turn in financial matters.

Colleagues

You will get most out of the staff if you can advocate and inspire rather than bully or threaten. In fact, if you empathise with those who feel threatened by the subject matter or methodology of history you could lead them gently towards a higher level of teaching competence than those who believe they have all the answers. The latter type of teacher needs a different kind of approach involving a constant dialogue about the best way to teach certain aspects of history. Often, engaging teachers in discussions about their practice in comparison with yours will broaden both of your outlooks and result in some accommodation of both points of view.

Governors

You will have a statutory duty to report to the governing body. Your communication skills will need to be adapted to take account of the variety of personnel on this body. They will all be interested in what you have to say so do not waste this opportunity to sell your subject.

Parents

The great demands made on children's time by the ten subjects plus RE may cause some parents to feel less than committed to their child doing history when he or she could be doing sums. You will need to sell your subject through the enthusiasm you exude, the keenness of your class and, perhaps if that is not working, through holding a workshop session for parents to see what history involves. It is also necessary in these financially constrained times to court the PTA. This group has fund raising capacities which could be put towards raising the resource level of your history provision or contributing towards a school visit to a historically important site.

The wider community

The Programmes of Study demand that at least one unit is based on local history and that oral history is one of the sources children use. In addition, they must use buildings and sites, documentary evidence, pictures and photographs and artefacts. It would be a crime if the people who live in the school's catchment area were to be ignored as first hand source material and repositories of evidence. Teachers are rather wary, for all sorts of reasons, of having other adults in their classrooms. You will need to show them, through your example, the benefits that can come from involving the local community in children's history work. It may be politic for you to do the local study unit in your classroom to show the staff how you plan and implement it using people from the neighbourhood. Your aim should be, however, to give another member of staff the unit as soon as they feel up to the challenge.

Strategies for staff development

You will be watched and listened to critically by other members of staff to see if you are worthy of the role of subject manager. Your ability as an inspirational class teacher will give you credibility in the eyes of your colleagues. If you are not such an inspirational teacher, you must work at it. Keep up a constant self-evaluation exercise, acknowledge your weak spots and do something about them through reflective analysis. It helps to have discussions with a critical friend who has watched you teach. Two heads are mostly better than one in these cases. If you are not comfortable with this idea you will understand the hesitancy of colleagues letting you into their rooms to watch them teach.

INSET

There can be little doubt that INSET can be one of the most powerful ways of influencing colleagues. Through INSET changes in knowledge, skills and attitudes can be started which will affect the quality of teaching and learning. Organising and running INSET are part of your job. As you will not have many opportunities for doing this, you must not waste this chance to stimulate colleagues' commitment to quality history teaching. The focus of a session will be negotiated by you with the staff. What are their major concerns about history teaching? Sort out the responses you get into groups under headings. This will help you hit more than one concern in a session. (Whole school planning is central to the history programme of study and will be dealt with in Parts 2 and 4). The use of resources to promote the historical skills of children may need to be a focus for an INSET activity. Too often, you will explain to the staff, artefacts are used inappropriately so that the children miss the chance of practising historical skills. Instead, they practise their artistic and observational skills as they record what they see through drawing, painting or modelling. Once you have set the rationale for why a session on using artefacts with children is useful, you must plan the session carefully, getting the timing and pace right and ensuring that there is something for everyone included. One way to do this is to always include the idea of progression and continuity to the activity. In this way, the Year 6 teacher and the Year 1 teacher, while working with the same objects, will be considering how to extend their chidren's expertise in historical investigation.

Artefacts session

Aims
You must clarify these to yourself so that the session is geared to the desired outcome.

Some aims for you to consider might include:

to give teachers an appreciation of the historical skills it is possible to practise on an object;

- to develop an aide memoire of these skills for teachers' history resource file;
- to develop a list of questions which may be used in class with children to help them focus on the major historical concepts of time, chronology, change and continuity, similarity and difference, empathy, cause and effect, power and consensus, and (the really important one) the nature of evidence;
- to look at one specific study unit from the point of view of resourcing it with artefacts;
- or to use one type of artefact (for example, light making objects) from different times to draw out the key concepts around which to develop questions.

Resourcing the session

Your aims will define your resourcing for this session. You may want to introduce the teachers to the idea of museum artefacts boxes at the same time. If so you will need to have ordered this from the museum. You may need to have prepared for this session by rereading Durbin et al.'s excellent book (1990) on using artefacts with children. We would advise that you do not use her worksheet exemplar with the teachers, useful as it is. Let the staff think about the need for a worksheet, its format and length in the light of their particular class's attainment levels.

Organising the session

Things to consider:
how are you going to introduce the session?
how long will it last?
how will you organise the staff — individually, in small groups, or by key stage?
how much time will you give to hands on experience, to discussion, to teaching (giving information etc.).

Possible uses of artefacts

There are a wide range of ways of using artefacts and objects to aid the development of historical enquiry. The 'Suitcase Game' is a worthwhile activity. Fill different bags with different types of objects, for example, items collected while on holiday. The aim is to find out as much as possible about the person whose bag it is. A way of ending a session like this is to confirm that all the bags contain objects that belong to you, and the guesses provided by each group of teachers are all equally valid — if they have the evidence to support them. In this way, it is possible to illustrate that history is an inexact subject. We cannot possibly know the truth about things; we can only make educated guesses based on evidence.

Photographs also provide considerable opportunity to develop questioning and enquiry. A good example of this is for each group of teachers to be given a photograph and asked to design ten questions about it. Five of the questions should be able to be answered by looking at the photograph; the other five should require a degree of inference. For example, a picture of a rock concert may provide questions such as 'How many flags can you see?' On the other hand, the question 'What year is it?' will require the teachers to use their skills and knowledge, as well as their historical awareness, to date the photograph.

What you need to do as a subject manager, is move teachers away from simply getting children to draw and describe artefacts, and towards using the artefacts to build on children's ability to question and inquire.

Expected outcomes

- Everyone will have enjoyed the experience.
- The teachers' repertory of strategies for teaching children history will have been refined in all cases.
- The list of questions will be ready for trial in classrooms.
- Colleagues will recognise the need for more artefacts.

There will be unexpected outcomes for you to capitalise on and which will inform the planning of your next INSET session.

INSET as an awareness raising activity

We use INSET at different times for different purposes. The need to be always alert to the inherent problems of trying to

Suggestion

To alert teachers to the central importance of carefully choosing the content and method of each study unit with equal opportunities in mind, it will be useful to carry out a couple of short activities.

keep a balance within our teaching of history is something you will need to bring to the attention of staff frequently. Balance is a big issue. Children are entitled to be taught about the lives of men and women and children in the past. This is very hard to achieve because of the lack of teacher knowledge of these aspects and because of the paucity of source material covering men, women and children. However, there is some material available and it needs to be found and incorporated into the various study units by the staff with your help. It is important for children's view of themselves and of the past that teachers take this search for material to give a fuller picture of the past seriously. There is a tendency for us to use the knowledge we learned at school as if it were the totality of what there is to know in history knowledge terms. You could discuss this with the staff when you do an INSET session with them to consider the issues of gender, multicultural education and their necessary inclusion in each Unit.

Activities investigating issues of equal opportunities

Activity 1

Put up a piece of string across the room and ask the staff to write down three names of people who lived in the past whom they would have liked to have met. Next, give them paper clips to attach these on the string 'time-line' in chronological sequence (identify which end of the string is the present and which one distant past). This exercise nearly always highlights the glaring omissions in the history teaching experienced by the participants. Men predominate, of course, with the addition of the inevitable Florence Nightingale and Boudicca. History is portrayed, when viewed from these lines, as the story of rich, powerful men in Britain and Europe. Thomas Carlyle's comment 'History is but the biography of famous men' may well be borne out by this exercise. People from other parts of the world are rarely mentioned, nor are children. It is useful to look at the purposes of school history when this exercise is completed. One of the purposes involves helping children to develop a sense of identity. Discuss with your colleagues whether their feelings of identity are heightened or marginalised by looking at the lines. If they feel less than happy with their view of themselves when looking at the people displayed, think how much bigger children's sense of exclusion from history will be.

Activity 2

How much do you or your colleagues know about the role of black people in our history?

Quiz

Which African country did the Roman unit stationed at Aballava (near Carlisle) come from in AD 210?

How many Indians enlisted for Britain in 1914?

The black trumpeter, John Blanke, was employed by which two English Kings?

What was Noor Inayat Khan's code name? Where did she work?

Name Britain's first Indian restaurant.

Which black person went 200 rounds with Tom Britton in 1836?

What event did Bristol celebrate with firework displays and a half day holiday in 1791?

Which soccer team did the black goalkeeper Arthur Wharton sign for in 1896?

Who was elected Britain's first Asian MP in 1892?

Stella Thomas was the first black woman to be called to the Bar. When?

The fact that most teachers will be unable to answer these questions may at first seem threatening. People do not like to be made brutally aware of their shortcomings. Approached in a non-threatening way, however, this exercise could demonstrate to your colleagues the missing people of history, and how some cultures, races and even to a large extent, a whole gender have been eliminated from our knowledge of what happened in the past. This would demonstrate a need for teachers to offer balance in their history, as best they can, building on support offered by you.

We do not know all there is to know about the history of Britain but that can never be a reason given for the history entitlement of children being unbalanced with the absence of some groups of people. Your job as subject manager of history is to heighten your colleagues' understanding that they have a commitment to providing children with some understanding of the variety of races and cultures that have gone into the making of present day Britain. It might be useful to discuss the proposition that everyone who lives in Britain today is an immigrant or the descendant of an immigrant. The fact is that resources can be found for this area of the curriculum though sometimes they are sparse. History, after all, is not the study of the past. To paraphrase G.R. Elton, history is the study of the present traces of the past. Some people's history is harder to find. This, in itself, is a worthwhile discussion point with staff.

This section on the organisation and use of INSET has concentrated on you as provider. There are very good videos you can use with staff to observe how children learn history in many different ways (English Heritage, see Resource Section). You can also use a visiting speaker to create extra interest as a change from you. The use of other members of staff to show how they have managed to provide their class with good quality teaching is something you should work hard to achieve. Discovering and nurturing effective practice within your school is one of the perks of the job.

A final thought

In our experience some teachers are known to object to INSET approaches where they become the children. On closer investigation, this actually means that they object to being treated like children. This can be avoided if you keep the activities on a professional level. For example, at the end of the artefacts session ask your colleagues if they have any examples from their history teaching which show the need for evidence. Discuss where the evidence comes from and how the children have access to it. This demonstrates to your colleagues that the task they have just performed was not simply an enjoyable one, but one which they can use to further their ability to teach and understand history more effectively.

Part two

What history coordinators need to know

Chapter 3

What history coordinators need to know

What must be taught in terms of studying history is now fairly simple. The National Curriculum provides the structure and framework of content in the subject, and as a legal requirement will obviously drive the planning and content of history in the primary classroom. However, the National Curriculum does not provide a subject manager with the detail needed to produce the kind of planning necessary in the modern classroom. Before we enter the murky realms of organising what the National Curriculum does provide us with, let us look first at the statutory requirements.

The National Curriculum for history

The slimline post-Dearing National Curriculum is a considerable improvement on the previous document in terms of the content required to be taught by the end of Key Stage 2.

In Key Stage 1, there remains one area of study, in effect a study unit, which consists of **three** separate strands.

1   Children should be taught about the everyday lives of men and women from the past. The Programme of Study states that children should be given the opportunity to investigate changes in their own lives and aspects of the way of life of people in Britain in a time beyond living memory.
2   Children should be taught about famous men and women, including personalities drawn from British history.
3   Finally, they should also be taught about past events and anniversaries, including events from the history of Britain. Examples given include religious festivals and the Gunpowder Plot.

In Key Stage 2, content increases dramatically. There are six study units, concerning various periods of time, with a definite focus on British History.

The areas that need to be studied are:
1   Romans, Anglo-Saxons and Vikings in Britain, choosing one of the three for a more in-depth study.
2   Life in Tudor times
3   Victorian Britain **OR** Britain since the 1930s.
4   Ancient Greece.
5   An aspect of local history.
6   A past non-European society, choosing from Ancient Egypt, Mesopotamia, the Indus Valley, the Maya, Benin or the Aztecs.

As well as this definition of content contained within the Programmes of Study, both Key Stages also have Key Elements, which provide an outline of the skills that children should acquire during their historical study.

1   Chronology
2   Range and depth of historical understanding and knowledge concerning the periods studied.
3   Being aware of different interpretations of history, and the reasons why these differences exist.
4   Historical enquiry using primary and secondary sources.
5   Organising and communicating their historical knowledge.

The Key Elements, coupled with the study units, are an attempt to provide a skeleton of schools history which the subject manager and staff must flesh out. The document is not the be all and end all of primary history, although its statutory nature does make it appear so. As will be shown, the document is an exceptionally flexible tool, which an able subject manger can use to provide the framework for excellent history within their school.

What it means for schools and the subject manager

Annotated briefly in the last section is the outline for the National Curriculum for history. The obvious implication for any school is that what is contained within its pages must be taught, therefore the job of the subject manager is to fit it all in, in a meaningful way. This requires a sound long term plan, detailing when each unit will be taught, or in the case of Key Stage 1, when each section of a unit will be taught. This does not cause any obvious problems, as most schools already have in place a long term plan, and most schools appear to teach the subject of history chronologically. This approach will be considered later. Firstly, there are problems that apply to individual schools that need to be looked at.

Mixed age classes

This must provide an organisational headache to any subject manager, and history is no different. The problem of repeating work, and re-studying areas already covered requires a different kind of planning to that of a school with no mixed classes. One possible solution was provided in the Non-statutory guidance that accompanied the original National Curriculum orders, and has been adapted here in the light of the Dearing Review. The planning runs in a two year cycle, to ensure coverage and to remove the chances of repetition.

Key Stage 2: Possible sequence of units in a mixed age class

1997	Years 3 and 4	Romans, Anglo-Saxons and Vikings in Britain
	Years 5 and 6	Britain since 1930s/The Victorians
1998	Years 3 and 4	Tudor Times and Non-European Society
	Years 5 and 6	Ancient Greece and Local Study Unit

This rolling two year cycle would alleviate the problem of repeating work, and provide a stable framework for teaching staff, who would be aware of their areas of study well in advance of having to teach them. Another approach has been witnessed as well, that of the whole school topic. Some schools are using this approach to ensure coverage of the units where there are a number of mixed classes. Basically, the whole school will work on a unit, although of course the work will vary in difficulty depending on the age of the children. This method does have some merits. It obviously negates the need for a two year rolling programme, and also fosters a tremendous community spirit throughout a school. We will look more closely at potential problems when we look at the need for progression across the Key Stage.

Timing the units

Some schools are having difficulty delivering the enormous bulk of content required in the National Curriculum, across ten different areas and RE. As a result they are attempting to cram in as many areas as possible into as short a space of time as possible. The problem with history is especially prevalent in Key Stage 2 where six units need to be taught in four years, as well as all the other subjects. We cannot promise that this book will help create time, but we can suggest to subject managers that history needs to be included at the forefront of the school's planning. Recent OFSTED reports in various schools have highlighted concerns that history managers need to be aware of. Gone are the days when history can be marginalised, or relegated, because of a lack of time. On the contrary, recent OFSTED evidence suggests that history's position of importance is quite safe, and they have reported on schools with this in mind. The key feature of several reports that we have come across has been the timing of the units, i.e., when the units are actually taught. For example, in one school, Year 3 children studied the Romans in depth in the first term, as their major history work for the year. History, as a subject was not touched again until the spring term of Year 4, when children studied the Tudors, followed by the Local Study Unit, which took account of the community's existence in Tudor times. OFSTED criticised the school for the length of time between study units, and the school had to replan its entire history curriculum to take this into account. Given that Key Stage 2 children are studying within school for a total of twelve terms, and that there are six study units, it seems reasonable to expect a history unit to appear on a fairly regular basis.

The school in question now teaches their study units as follows:		
Term One:	(Y3)	Romans, Anglo-Saxons and Vikings in Britain
Term Three:	(Y3)	Ancient Greeks
Term Five:	(Y4)	A Non-European Society
Term Seven:	(Y5)	Tudor Life
Term Eight:	(Y5)	Local Study Unit
Term Ten:	(Y6)	Britain since the 1930s

This seems to more than satisfy the need to provide history on a regular basis throughout the Key Stage. The upheaval that resulted from the school's OFSTED report was considerable, and avoidable. Subject managers need to be very aware of the timing of the study units.

Single subject or cross curricular?

This is a never ending debate that rears its head from time to time, normally when the standards of history teaching are called into question. It again goes back to the perhaps even older debate about time. History as a foundation subject should, according to Dearing's recommendations, be taught, on average, for an hour and a quarter a week throughout the year. What needs to be made clear here is that Dearing's recommendations are exactly that, mere recommendations. They are not a statutory requirement. However, if we approach the subject as if there was a one hour a week requirement, then we can see instantly the illusion of ease that simply timetabling one and a quarter hours a week, say 10.45 until 12.00 on a Wednesday morning, can provide. Hooray, we hear schools cry, that's our history sorted, now, when shall we timetable our art? If only life were that simple. An immediate question which raises its head is whether the children will be able to remember the previous week's teaching! The problem that then exists is teaching a subject that permeates all the other subjects as an exclusive area of study. The potential then exists for a return to the type of history that dominated our schools in the past — copying pages from textbooks, colouring in pictures and answering meaningless questions about unconnected stories.

History is not a subject that can be taught as an exclusive. To teach history well requires that children are aware of all the areas of their life that history touches, from the origins of the mathematics they are working on, to their right to a free education. This is not something that can be taught in isolation over one session a week. As we shall see when we discuss planning individual study units, to teach history in isolation would be a horrible waste of a universal discipline.

Planning the subject: different ways of approaching history

Long term planning: study units

There is a need for the history subject manager to produce, in co-operation with the staff, a long term plan for the school. This plan should be produced bearing in mind what we have already discussed concerning the timing of the units in Key Stage 2 and the problems that are related to a mixed age classes. The order in which the study units should be taught is not prescribed, so the school can choose when each individual unit will make an appearance. In Key Stage 1, there is an important need to ensure that each one of the three strands of the area of study receives attention throughout the Key Stage.

These can best be achieved through quite prescriptive long term planning, along the lines of

Reception: A topic on Ourselves, that includes work on the child, the child's family, concentrating on those areas mentioned in the Programmes of Study, including clothes, diet, houses, jobs.

Year 1: Using the local area study in geography to study old buildings, transportation, and entertainment, leading on to what life would have been like for a child when one of the old buildings was first built.

Year 2: A topic on festivals, that can cover religious festivals, anniversaries and specific events, such as the Olympic Games.

As you will no doubt have picked up, we have shied away from detailing famous people that can be studied. There is a desperate need in history to ensure that balance is provided, for all people regardless of race, gender or religion. The Key Stage 1 area of study does not specify which famous people should be taught, although it does provide a 'helpful' list of areas that could be considered, including rulers, saints, artists engineers, explorers, inventors and pioneers. A brief glance at the list will show that these areas, if followed by a school, could result in history being about white, Christian men. This is a danger that needs to be rectified at school level. There needs to be due consideration to famous women in these areas of study, and to famous blacks. History is a powerful tool that helps to shape the way in which we think. There needs to be a balance across the Key Stage. If women account for roughly 50 per cent of the population, then they should also account for a very large percentage of the famous people that are studied. As we discussed in the chapter about INSET, this is an area where considerable improvements need to be made in schools. It is the responsibility of the subject manager to ensure that proper attention is given to this when detailing which personalities should be covered by staff.

Possible examples that could be used include people such as Mary Seacole or even modern day heroes such as Nelson Mandela and Desmond Tutu. There needs to be a cross section of society represented when schools consider which famous people to include in their historical studies, and it is the subject manager who should ensure that a balance exists.

Things to consider when placing study units
- timing of the unit;
- resources;
- staff knowledge (Ancient Greece for the teacher who visited Greece in the summer, for example, or an area previously taught);
- staff enthusiasm for certain areas (Britain since 1930s, for example, may be a popular choice for some staff);
- possibility of suitable trips to historical sites.

At Key Stage 2, the problems are quite different, because of the more restrictive nature of the study units. The advice offered to schools on the production of the first National Curriculum for history was eagerly seized upon by large numbers of schools. It seemed to be that the advice that was offered went unchallenged, despite the fact that it has absolutely no grounding in any historical research of which we are aware. We are, of course, referring to the teaching of the study units in chronological order, a point seemingly taken for granted by the original Non-statutory Guidance. A huge number of schools teach the units that are concerned with the history of Britain in chronological order, starting in Year 3 with the Romans, Anglo-Saxons and Vikings in Britain, moving onto the Tudors, and ending with either Britain since the 1930s or the Victorians. Some schools will even teach all six units in chronological order, perhaps taking such a decision after seeing the Non-statutory Guidance, with its immortal line that if the children were not taught the units in chronological order, they 'could see history as a confusing jumble of events'. Unfortunately, such a claim is utter rubbish, and totally unfounded. There is no research anywhere, to the best of our knowledge, that suggests that teaching events in chronological order cements the notion of chronology in the minds of children.

When teaching a Year 4 class about the Ancient Greeks, the concept with which they struggled the most was chronology. There were very few children in the class who clearly grasped the fact that the events being taught took place 2500 years ago. For a while their work was filled with historical anachronism, such as electricity and wrist watches! For the least able children, Ancient Greece was on another planet, which bore no relation to their own, and teaching in chronological order was not going to help. What was needed was something concrete, something they would understand. Eventually, our work became focused on modern Greece, as a tourist centre, and the children had to plan which sites they wanted their 'tour parties' to visit. They had to investigate the sites, helped by old holiday photographs and brochures, and produce booklets about each site that they wished to visit. This at least was an attempt to ensure that what we were doing held some relevance to the everyday lives of the children, rather than a jumble of abstract stories, places and names. The point seemed to be, and it is a point borne out by observing children being taught history, and attempting to understand what they are being taught, that the younger the child, the less life experience they have, and the less capable they are of the kind of abstract thought that is required when studying a culture that is completely alien to their own.

As a historian, it makes considerably more sense to start to teach history at the sharp end, as it were, with things that the children either know about themselves or can find out about fairly easily, through the adults around them. If we are to make history a living, breathing subject, which is relevant to the everyday lives of the children who are studying it, then where better to start than with the children and their families. The most accessible unit of all of the study units is Britain since the 1930s. This is a unit where the best resources of all are the living kind — people. Having seen this unit taught in both Year 3 and Year 6, it must be said that from the point of view of developing historical skills, the aim of the Key Elements in the National Curriculum, it was much more skills focused at Year 3. The children had to compile questions that they would like the answers to about life during the Second World War, and how it was both different and the same as life now.

The teacher had forged links between the school and a local old peoples' home, and it was there that the children went to find out the answers, straight from the horse's mouth, as it were. Everyone has a story to tell, and everyone's life is necessarily different from the next person's. The wealth of information that the children received, concerning both the Home Front and the fighting, was breathtaking. Perhaps even more impressively, the children recorded some of the interviews, and proudly informed the interviewees that their stories would be kept forever at an Oral History Bank that they were making at the school. The children were switched on to history, because it was there in front of them. They could ask questions, and find out what they needed to know, simply by communicating with other people. The class in question went on to use the sources they had now acquired to cover all the Key Elements, and many of the children carried their history into the home, asking the adults around them for the memories and thoughts that make each of us a historical resource.

This is good history, and the accessibility of the unit makes Britain since the 1930s an excellent one on which to start to build up children's historical skills, so that they are able to use them when studying much more difficult units, well beyond their living memory. These units should be taught at the very end of Key Stage 2, after the child has undergone a number of years of 'training' in the basic skills of the subject. In our opinion, a model which schools could adopt, which would be much more solidly based on research findings about how children learn history, is as follows —

Year 3: Britain since the 1930s
Year 4: The Tudors/Past Non-European Society
Year 5: Romans, Anglo-Saxons and Vikings in Britain
Year 6: Ancient Greece/Local Study Unit

We have placed the Local Study Unit in Year 6, as a well-planned local study would provide the chance for children to use the skills that have been built up over the previous three years, and act as historians within a familiar environment. However, it is an equally valid unit to attach onto Year 3, as the familiarity of the area may help to cement some of the concepts of history, such as the need for source material and the notion of similarity and difference and continuity and change.

The Local Study Unit is exceptionally flexible, and should be utilised in the most historically useful way. For example, a school in York could use the town's Viking history, and the resources that are available in the city, to link their Local History study to the unit about Romans, Anglo-Saxons and Vikings, in Year 5. Sadly we don't all teach in areas that contain large archaeological sites, or hold important positions in the history of Britain. We shall look at possible options when teaching the Local Study Unit for schools without obvious historical sites of interest close by in our section on planning a History Study Unit.

Medium term planning: what to look for in a study unit

After the school has decided which study units will be taught in which year groups, the teaching staff involved will need guidance as to how to plan a term or half term's work about a certain area. Chapter 5 provides detailed guidance about how to initiate and evaluate a specific history unit, in this case, the Ancient Greeks from the viewpoint of managing the subject. But we will briefly look at how you could advise teaching staff to approach any of the study units.

The first, most obvious point of reference is the Programme of Study for whichever unit is being taught. The content that needs to exist within the planning is contained within the National Curriculum, and should be followed. A brief look at any of the study units will show that teachers have a very large slice of freedom when planning the units. Statutory content requirement is actually quite limited, for example, in Life in Tudor Times, a statutory requirement is to look at the 'ways of life in town and country'. Effectively the Programme of Study points a teacher in the right direction, but lets them make their own way from then on. 'Ways of life in town and country' is a mammoth area, but because of the extremely limited prescription, a teacher can approach any area of this that they like, whether it be from the angle of employment or education. With such freedom comes responsibility. It would be very easy to simply teach the units as history has been taught in the past, and as it is continually taught in some schools (especially those with subject specific timetables), and get out the text books and start answering the questions. This is where the alarm bells should be ringing, and a history subject manager can turn the staff back to the other vital, and perhaps most important, aspect of the history National Curriculum. Turn to the Key Elements, and ask whether history taught exclusively from textbooks for one hour a week can possibly hope to cover the areas laid down as statutory requirements. We have seen history planned both ways, using primarily the study unit information, and also using the Key Elements. As we will detail in Chapter 5, the difference in the quality of history was very little, despite the differences in the planning procedures (see Chapter 4, p. 54). However, both units were planned alongside a history specialist, who had background knowledge concerning the Ancient Greeks, but very little knowledge of the area that was being studied in the Local History Unit. It is much easier to plan history when you have sufficient background knowledge of what you are studying. The plans for the Ancient Greece Unit were fairly straight forward, because the history specialist knew which areas could be covered, and which historical skills could be used when studying them. The Local Study Unit was a different kettle of fish entirely. With no knowledge base, the general consensus was to fall back to the absolute basics — the skills. The unit was planned by fitting activities around the skills, and the unit worked successfully.

Attention has been paid to the children acquiring historical skills. The subject is no longer content based, with a concentration on the acquiring of facts. If teachers are in doubt when producing a medium term plan, as subject manager, you should suggest using the Key Elements as guidance, and ensure that the skills that are mentioned within the Elements are catered for in some way during the unit.

The Key Elements should also provide the most important part of the medium term plan, the identified learning objectives, or what the teacher expects their children to learn from the study unit. As we will discuss in Part 3, the learning objectives should be assessible, and should contain reference to the Key Elements. There is little point assuming that an end of topic test is going to suffice for meaningful assessment, and so somewhere in the medium term plan should be reference to which skills the teacher is going to concentrate on, and then assess their children in. This should be referenced in the school's scheme of work, or if the scheme of work has not been written, then these learning objectives, which the subject manager must oversee, could form the basis of the school specific scheme of work as shown in Chapter 9. For example, in Year 1, using a local history approach, the teacher could include in the medium term planning reference to a learning objective along the lines of —

 The children can identify differences between ways of life at different times [Key Element]
Task — Using photographs of the local high street now and in the past, children can identify a number of differences, such as no cars, fewer people, etc.

This is a clearly identifiable learning objective. The teacher is declaring that by the end of the work that the class is doing, all the children should be able to state a number of differences between the old and new high street. The learning objective is skills based, not content based, and is lifted directly from the Key Stage 1 Programme of Study. We will consider the use of Key Elements in this way in more depth in Part Three.

Short term planning: ensuring coverage

The task of a short term plan, if medium term planning is produced properly, with identified learning objectives, is to ensure that what needs to be covered in the unit is covered. There will no doubt be considerable numbers of words written, to add to those already in existence, extolling the virtues of detailed short term planning, on a weekly basis, if not daily.

As a teacher, engaged in the teaching of eleven different subjects, dealing with, in some cases, classes of 35+, daily planning can be wasteful and not particularly useful. To produce detailed lesson objectives for every lesson can be viewed as, quite frankly, an insult to the professionalism of teachers. Detailed medium term planning, as discussed above, with relevant learning objectives in place, negate the need to spend two hours a night ploughing through the National Curriculum looking for relevant Level descriptions. The task of short term planning is to ensure that differentiation takes place and that each child in the class is occupied in a meaningful way, and perhaps, in the case of schools with more than single form entry, to ensure a parity of education throughout a year group. Perhaps the easiest way to illustrate the uses of medium and short term planning, with their relevance to the effective management of the subject and their place in a history unit is to use a specific example, and this is what we have done in Chapter 5.

Chapter 4

Teaching and learning history

The freedom offered by the National Curriculum, in terms of approaches to, and in a large degree, content of the study units, means that subject managers must be able to provide the guidance on teaching history that the statutory document fails to do. In the creation of the first history National Curriculum, the arguments between process and content were enormous, and nearly engulfed the Working Group. There are those who would hark back to a mythical 'Golden Age' of history, where each child could recite, parrot fashion, the events of 1066, and the wives of Henry VIII. These people would prefer a content-based history, where the 'fact' is all important, and history is presented as a series of dates, names and places to be absorbed and referred to. Unfortunately for these people, this is only a small part of the subject called history.

The key words in history are surely, take everything with a pinch of salt. This rather overturns the rote learning of facts, because of the need to determine what is a fact. This is the job of history — to try to establish fact, in the sure knowledge that someone, somewhere will disagree. History is, indeed, argument without end. Partly because of the incompleteness of our picture of the past, we can all argue about the relative importance, reliability and partiality of the evidence.

You will be amazed at the number of secondary school children who still believe everything they read in a school textbook, because it is from school, and school books don't tell lies. It is

Think about

History is an investigative subject, a subject of inquiry and argument. Most of all, history is opinion. To present opinion as fact may work wonders for the press, but is hardly the basis for a sound, inquisitive readership.

Think about

What needs to be taught within the subject of history is a questioning approach, where nothing is taken for granted.

the job of primary history to plant the seeds of enquiry and question, and the job of secondary schools to build on this.

It is absolutely vital that you carry the staff with you on what the fundamental aims of school history are. These were enshrined in the original National Curriculum Non-statutory Guidance and need to be the focus of staff discussion time before anything else can be done. To place them at the forefront of all subject development is a major task because we all have views about what history is and these are inevitably coloured by the way we were taught the subject — dates, kings, queens, politicians and the movers and shakers of times past. So, to remind you of the aims so that you can argue for a way to teach history that will satisfy them both:

There are two main aims of school history:
to help the pupils develop a sense of identity through learning about the development of Britain, Europe and the world;

to introduce pupils to what is involved in understanding and interpreting the past.

Each purpose is worthy of discussion with the staff. If this is done, the purposes will not remain theoretical statements of good intent, but become translated into achievable objectives with classes of children in mind. How can you as a history subject manager help staff to help their children develop a sense of identity through learning about Britain, Europe and the world? Does it feed a child's sense of identity to be told about the Ancient Greeks, the Egyptians, the Tudors or the Victorians? Not necessarily. It can be achieved only by you helping the staff to make links between the children's experience now with those of people in the past. The second aim involves the child in using the skills of the historian. These need to be understood and acknowledged by the staff so that they can be taught and developed with their classes. It is by engaging in this sort of discussion with the staff that they will appreciate that simple transmission of history facts is not what the primary history teacher is about. History as process involves us in examination of sources and interpretations in a critical appraising way to generate theories about their validity and reliability. Your main aim in staff development is to get consensus within the staff that history methodology is characterised by scrupulous respect for evidence and disciplined use of the imagination. From that consensus will follow teaching strategies and resource implications.

The approach that your school uses for teaching history should concentrate on the children finding out, and the children being taught to question what is taken for granted. This necessarily utilises primary source material, and the building of justifiable opinions by children. A briefest glance at the Key Elements will show that a questioning approach, adopted throughout a school, would almost certainly cover the range and depth of historical knowledge and understanding, interpretations of history, and historical enquiry. More importantly, teachers would be preparing their children for life in a society which increasingly presents opinions as facts, and half truths as gospel. First, we will look at two different approaches that we have witnessed in schools to teaching history in a way that complies with the National Curriculum.

The use of textbooks and schemes to teach history

When the National Curriculum first appeared, it was followed fairly swiftly by a plethora of schemes and published texts to 'aid' teachers in their struggles to fit everything in. This published scheme approach has continued, with schemes available from all the major publishing houses in every National Curriculum area. They are a kind of security blanket, grasped by teachers who are not confident in certain areas, or schools who lack experience in teaching certain subjects. History is one of those areas. As we have shown, history was barely taught in schools prior to the introduction of the National Curriculum, so it seemed natural for schools to grasp at resources offered to them from major, respected publishing houses. These schemes may have become the basis of your school's history curriculum, and if they have then this section will help you to evaluate whether or not you are actually even teaching history.

Dramatic as the last sentence may seem, it is a fact that some schools tend to concentrate less on actual history and more on English comprehension exercises. This is a real problem with scheme-based teaching of a subject that demands the use of primary source material and makes a statutory requirement of the use of documents, pictures, photographs, music, buildings and sites. Many textbooks are now lavishly illustrated, but the use of the illustrations leaves a lot to be desired. For example, one hugely successful scheme has a set of core textbooks for children that on the surface look wonderful. There are a large number of illustrations of primary sources, and some attempt to produce relevant pictures for passages of text, for example, a Roman carving of a battle in a section concerning Boudicca's revolt. The pictures normally have some questions attached, that are supposed to focus children's attention on the sources.

All of these features must have seemed like heavensent to some schools, who eagerly snapped up the scheme in question. Now comes the bad news, and should send subject managers scurrying to their own textbooks to check the content provided, and should also lead to some staff being enlightened about the proper use of schemes. The textbook in question, which looks at the Romans, Anglo-Saxons and Vikings fails to escape from the patronising view that children need to be spoon fed history.

There is no attempt made to provide the children with the chance to question any conclusions that the book jumps to. One example states 'Boudicca was angry . . . she said they had no right to do this,' when discussing the reasons for the Revolt.

How do the authors know this? They don't, they are just offering an opinion, but presenting it as a fact. This is a flaw that can be rectified by an awareness from teachers that it exists, but a lot of teachers are unaware of it themselves, and so add unwittingly to the wealth of opinion, not fact, that children are offered. The pictures, high quality illustrations of primary source material which schools will not have access to, are occasionally ruined by falsehoods such as 'This is what happened', when plainly it is not.

If television news crews can beam pictures around the world instantly, and these pictures be bent into a story loaded with bias and cultural precepts, such as the reporting of some

Think about

The sources do not represent **the** truth, they represent **someone's** truth.

events in Bosnia recently, then just think of the bias and cultural precepts that a wood carver or a stone mason can bring to bear on work that may take months to complete.

All history books have the prejudices of the writer either implicitly or explicitly stated, and to a large extent many primary sources are exactly the same. A good example of this is provided within the same pupil's book. There is an account of the Battle of Maldon, which lasts six pages, and on the surface appears to be an excellent account of the battle. Looking a little deeper, however, we can see that the only available source for the Battle of Maldon is Saxon. There is very little reference to this in the text, and the narrative that describes the battle is yet again presented as fact, when in fact the account being used may be a primary source, but it can hardly be described as impartial! This would be acceptable if the authors of the book had offered children the chance to decide for themselves whether or not they consider the source to be fair, but they stay silent.

It is with these faults in mind that we view textbook-based history teaching as flawed. The history being taught becomes only as good as the textbook, and if the authors offer opinion as fact, provide poor historical background and give little chance for children to become skilled in the art of history, then the history being taught will not be particularly inspiring.

An OFSTED discovery that has taken some schools by surprise has been the definition of history that teams have used when inspecting. The inspection teams of which we are aware have tended to concentrate their energies on discovering whether or not schools are providing proper attention to the Key Elements, and the skills of history, rather than the more mechanical side of the subject, which centres on the writing of information. The writing of information, the use of 'missing words', the neat presentation of historical stories is English — not history. This has caught many schools out, and led to criticism because schools actually are not teaching the subject in sufficient depth. If a school is using a textbook-centred approach to the subject, they can be faulted for being too superficial in their coverage, because of the skimpy and sometimes erroneous nature of the books, as we have discussed above. The questions

What to look for in a history textbook
- use of a number of alternative sources;
- child friendly text, that is factual and informative;
- opinion presented as opinion, 'I think, they thought';
- factual labels of illustrations — who, when, where — let the children discover what and why;
- questions that focus on historical knowledge and understanding — not just simple detail in the illustrations;
- fair representation of race and gender where appropriate.

asked by OFSTED across any school being inspected is whether or not the children progress, and how the school is measuring that progress. The development of children's factual knowledge is only one area of the Key Elements — schools need to satisfy all areas. If your school is not covering the Key Elements sufficiently, not only are you open to criticism from outside the school, from perhaps OFSTED or even parents, but you are also not addressing the most important aspect of your teaching — the provision of quality learning experiences which will see your pupils make progress. As subject manager, it is of crucial importance that you ensure that the children in your school are provided with the opportunities to make progress across the whole range of historical skills — not just their knowledge. It is not good enough to plough through a textbook, ignoring the fundamental nature of history, that of investigation, enquiry, and questioning. Without these aspects, and without some reference to children acquiring the skills of historians, schools are indeed teaching English, where they should be teaching history.

There is a need for you to work with staff so that they use their discussion and questioning time to develop their children's historical skills — even when they are at a site of historical interest, the questioning may not be historically focused. For example, children may be looking at a building and noting such things as number and types of windows, the materials used in its construction and making a count of the people using it. This is fine as an information gathering exercise. To get the children thinking historically, however, the teacher has to get them to ask such questions as:

- How old is the building? (Time)
- Has it changed in any way since it was built? (Continuity/Change)
- Why have the changes occurred? (Cause/Consequence)
- Can you put the changes in chronological order? (Sequence)
- Is the building like the others near it? (Similarity/Difference)
- Why was it built, and why has it survived? (Historical Understanding)
- What evidence have you to support your conclusions? (Analysing the relative strengths of the evidence gathered to support the judgment)
- Is the evidence sufficient, reliable or conflicting?

Using the Key Elements to teach history

Rather than using what a textbook could offer, we will show how one school approached the problem of teaching a Local Study Unit, as a free standing topic, for the first time. The teachers involved had no real knowledge of the area that they would study, and had no textbook to fall back on. For the trained historian involved it was an experience akin to a non-historian approaching any of the study units, and in that sense, it may be useful to share with readers the approach that was adopted, so that, as the subject manager, you could offer it as a possible solution to any planning problems your colleagues may face in history.

First, all the possible resources were collected together, including letters and county council documents detailing the planning and building of the school, books by local historians, old school records including photographs, and a collection of old maps. Then the focus of the study was decided on, referring to the Programme of Study for guidance. It was decided that the aspect to be studied should be the provision of education over a period of time, including the building and re-building of the school (it was burnt down during the last decade). This was where the planning meeting ground to a halt. Not enough was known about the subject for any of the teachers involved to start giving examples of possible classroom activities. So it appeared that the topic was a non-starter and would be one of those topics that takes an age to get into, and never really gets anywhere. However, the suggestion then came from the history subject manager to refer back to the Key Elements, and see which skills needed to be utilised by the children.

A brief guide to the Key Elements

- Chronology — The placing of events studied within a time scale.
- Range and depth of historical understanding — Cause and consequence, similarity and difference. Not just knowing who, where and when, but why.
- Interpretations of history — Why are events shown in a certain way? What has happened for an event or person to be represented in this way? Is the representation accurate?

■ Historical enquiry	Using sources, both primary source material and secondary sources.
■ Organisation and communication	How children demonstrate their historical knowledge and understanding.

Here the planning began to take shape, as you can see:

Skill: chronology

Placing events in a chronological framework was to be fairly straightforward. A timeline would be built up, using the opening dates and closing dates of various schools in the area (which could be found out in a local history book) to provide a history of educational provision. Allied with this, the children would build up their own timelines, asking grandparents, parents, or guardians for information about when they attended school, which school, and for how long. This would also involve the skill of historical enquiry, using adults as a primary source. Using dates and terms relating to the passing of time could also be covered because of the growth of the area during Victorian times, so it was decided that as well as a 'schools' timeline, there should also be a 'major events' line, where the teachers would choose events of major historical significance and add these to the top of the 'schools' time line. The creation of the children's own personal timelines seemed an obvious starting point for the topic, and became the first activity that was done.

Skill: range and depth of historical understanding

How to study the characteristic features of an indefinible period of time that was to be covered was a potential problem, but one that was overcome by concentrating on school life in previous years. The teachers had to be fairly cautious, as the children also studied the Victorians in Year 6, with a significant period of time spent on school life in this period. Obviously then, this was one area that could not be studied any more than briefly, and it was decided that the main concentration would be on school in the time of parents or grandparents, and how it differed from now. Areas to be looked at would include different classrooms, subjects and teachers, and a look at punishments, as the children were fascinated by the thought of rulers, canes and dunces' caps. Again the main resource was to be adults that the children were in contact with.

The teachers themselves became a resource, with their memories of school as different as their ages (from 23 to 40), and the school secretary was invaluable, as she had actually attended the school as a pupil. The planning included the chance for the children to interview her as part of a 'fact finding' mission, that would include other long serving members of staff, and the headteacher. There was also the opportunity to create an oral history bank of interviews, where the children would decide which of the adults were worth recording, in terms of the usefulness of their recollections. As there was a concentration on school life, making a link between periods studied was fairly straightforward, as school had been around for a while!

It was the second part of this Key Element, the skill of describing and identifying reasons for and results of historical events, that looked to be the most difficult to cover. Given that the school was built after the Second World War, it was decided to concentrate on why the school had been built (a local population boom) and, on studying the documents relating to the building of the school, it was discovered that the land was previously a small farm, and there was a document relating to the need to delay the building, because the land was needed for food production. When the school was eventually constructed, the land that is now the playing field was left as part of the farm for as long as possible. It was decided that the children would have to research why the land was so valuable that even a school was of less importance.

Skill: interpretations of history

This is perhaps the most difficult skill of the Key Elements, and one that it was decided to steer clear of in this study unit. It is a skill that requires some conflict of source material, as you will see from the planning of the Ancient Greece unit detailed in Chapter 5. As primary source material was scarce, and there was no real conflict contained within it, this was a skill that could not be covered properly. The subject manager would have to ensure that this area was covered sufficiently in other study units that the children were to be taught.

Skill: historical enquiry

There was already considerable historical enquiry planned for, with the children being asked to interview various adults to find out about their memories of school. However, as there was a recent dramatic and historical event, the burning down of the original school building, it was decided that the children would also be asked to study the various sources that were available, from photographs of the old school burning down to the newspaper reports in the local press, as well as the memories of older brothers or sisters (of which there were several) who attended the school at the time and a series of pieces of creative writing from the oldest juniors, at the school at the time of the fire, about their reactions to it. It was decided that with the wealth of resources about this specific event, the children would be asked to construct a newspaper report about the fire and its aftermath, including the building of the new school building. The children were also able to use one of the more under-used areas of this Key Element, the use of buildings and sites, as some of the school survived, and old foundation lines were still visible in the playground. The plan was to have the subject manager talk to the children, and walk them around the 'old' site, a sort of guided tour, to increase the children's understanding of the layout of the old school, so that they could compare it directly with the rebuilt school.

Skill: organisation and communication

It was decided to concentrate on children communicating their knowledge in different ways. These included 'diaries' of children at school at the same time as the adults that the children had interviewed, a newspaper report of the fire and its effects, a description of the old school, including a plan of the layout, and the listing of differences between the children's school days and those of their interviewees, as well as the similarities.

As you can see, by switching attention away from the factual knowledge of a study unit and towards the skills required to be a historian, these teachers managed to construct an extremely worthwhile history topic which would enable the children to acquire historical skills. This plan will no doubt be adapted next year, as the teachers will have taught the topic and have more knowledge of the factual side of the unit but the approach in planning will be very similar. It was decided, in the original History National Curriculum, to include a unit that would study the immediate locality and require the children to use the skills of historians when studying it. Why approach the unit then from any other angle but the angle of original intention — the skills, not the facts. It is not necessary to view textbooks as the only possible option to being confidently secure in a subject area, as this approach shows. All that is needed is reference to the Key Elements, and activities that are related to these skills, and the study unit starts to build itself, in a way that would satisfy the statutory requirements of the National Curriculum, and present children with the opportunities to be historians, and discover information for themselves, and work out how to use it, a skill not just necessary for history, but for life as well.

As subject manager, such an approach could be presented to your colleagues, as this would ensure from the planning, through to the implementation of the study unit in the classroom, that there was sufficient attention to the Key Elements, and therefore to the progression of the children as historians, with the skills necessary to study the subject effectively.

Chapter 5

Planning and teaching history

As the history subject manager, you will need to encourage staff to plan and teach history to as high a standard as possible. Bearing in mind that teachers have different methods for doing this, this chapter gives you the opportunity to look at a model approach to planning and teaching history. You may find this useful both from the standpoint of evaluating your own methodology and that of the teachers with whom you work. The aim of this chapter is to encourage you to consider the method of history planning throughout your school. We are well aware that most schools have in place a planning structure of some form, and some people may feel it unwise to tamper with a set structure, but as you will see from the chapter, most of the changes that you would need to make, in order not only to ensure documentation exists of your school's coverage of the history National Curriculum, but to make the task of establishing an accurate scheme of work much easier, are minimal. Our aim is not to increase the amount of paperwork involved, but work towards decreasing it.

By focusing on one study unit, and developing our ideas through it, we hope to show that implementing effective history is not as difficult or as daunting as it appears at first. Our planning model can obviously be adapted for any study unit, as you will see.

Using the study units to implement the National Curriculum

Now that we have discussed possible approaches to implementing history in your school, it is time to look at how to use the study units to ensure coverage of the National Curriculum and high quality history teaching within your school. You have a responsibility to provide coverage of the whole document, not simply part of it. That means that you, as subject manager, have to ensure that every area of the document is being covered throughout the school. How can this be managed? First, and most importantly, a practical scheme of work, based on what is actually happening in your school, highlighting the best practice, and helping to raise the standard of history throughout the school, will be your most important document to show that the school covers the National Curriculum. In this chapter regarding implementing a scheme of work, we offer some practical ideas on how to start what seems to be a very difficult task. We also look at how to monitor the scheme of work, and adapt it when the need arises, as it surely will.

The next area to consider when looking to ensure that the National Curriculum is taught in your school is the planning, probably over the medium term. We would assume that every school has allocated areas of the history study units to year groups, or, if adopting a whole school topic approach, has organised a time table of study for each of the units. Some history subject managers may believe that that is their job done. This is simply not the case. The briefest glance at the document shows that each study unit in Key Stage 2 is broken down into specific areas of study, and at Key Stage 1 the study unit may consist of three strands, but each of the strands has its own statutory requirements. For example, strand two includes the needs to teach different kinds of famous men and women, including personalities from British history. This has a large number of possibilities. At Key Stage 1, every school, to ensure proper coverage of the National Curriculum for history should be teaching:

1   Lives of famous men of different kinds
2   Lives of famous women of different kinds
3   Lives of famous British men of different kinds
4   Lives of famous British women of different kinds

FIG 5.1
Medium term plan for history at
Key Stage 2: Ancient Greeks

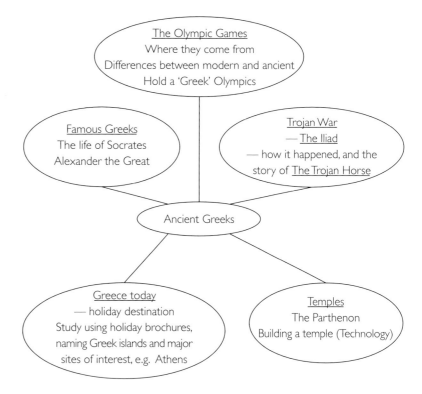

The Olympic Games
Where they come from
Differences between modern and ancient
Hold a 'Greek' Olympics

Famous Greeks
The life of Socrates
Alexander the Great

Trojan War
— The Iliad
— how it happened, and the
story of The Trojan Horse

Ancient Greeks

Greece today
— holiday destination
Study using holiday brochures,
naming Greek islands and major
sites of interest, e.g. Athens

Temples
The Parthenon
Building a temple (Technology)

Taken to its extreme, assuming that 'different kinds' comes to the fore, this could cover the lives of upwards of a dozen different people. This shows that the existence of only one study unit at Key Stage 1 does not make its coverage easier, just more vague. The medium term planning becomes crucial — and OFSTED will pore over the medium term planning documents of any school to find coverage of the National Curriculum. It is, perhaps, one of the most easily avoided pitfalls of an inspection, because the document is absolutely clear in what needs to be studied within each unit. Let us look at an example of a medium term plan for the Ancient Greeks at Key Stage 2 (see Figure 5.1). This is a plan which looks like a fairly realistic attempt to limit the topic area while still achieving some coverage. Some subject managers may even recognize the style of the plan as one similar to their own school's. At the risk of being prophets of doom, this plan is wholly inadequate, and would hopefully be seen as such by you as history subject manager.

If this is the type of plan teachers produce in your school, it is necessary for you to work with them to show how to refine and develop it until it is sufficient. One way of doing this is to follow the procedure described next. Let us break the plan down and see why it is inadequate, and then produce a plan of the same study unit which would satisfy the statutory requirements of the document, and the demands and rigours of an OFSTED inspection, as well as the all important need to ensure the progression and development of historical skills in the children in your school.

The first notable feature of the plan is the lack of reference to the National Curriculum, a feature which would, and should, be instantly recognised by you as history subject manager. There is a need at the medium term planning level to refer constantly to the document from which, after all, a teacher is supposed to find what they are required to do. In the centre of the plan how much extra time would it have taken to have written 'Ancient Greeks, Key Stage 2 History, Study Unit 4'? Yet, this simple addition would immediately show a reference to the document which is, quite simply, crucial.

The areas of study chosen by the teacher(s) who wrote this plan seem to provide a broad coverage of the topic. The Olympic Games, the Trojan Wars, temples, famous Greeks and Greece today are all areas worthy of being taught, and all areas likely to appeal to the children. Unfortunately, these areas are not tied to the Programmes of Study contained within the study unit, and, if you are to ensure coverage, this is what has to be done. The areas shown on the original plan have to be 'adapted' to fit into the study unit's requirements, and it must be shown that what is taught covers the unit. This is not as difficult as it first appears. With the exception of the area involving Greece today, everything else on the plan can be filled into the study unit. What is needed is acknowledgment of the use of the document, again, to show reference to the statutory requirements. For example, instead of writing 'The Olympic Games', the heading for that particular section should be 'PoS,e': Influence on the modern world'. As soon as the areas to be studied are assigned to Programmes of Study within the study unit, it becomes apparent that there is a glaring omission, which is not readily identifiable on the original medium plan. If this course of study was to be taken, then the children would not study Athens or Sparta — and this is a statutory requirement. While

FIG 5.2
Medium term plan of KS2 History
referring to study unit

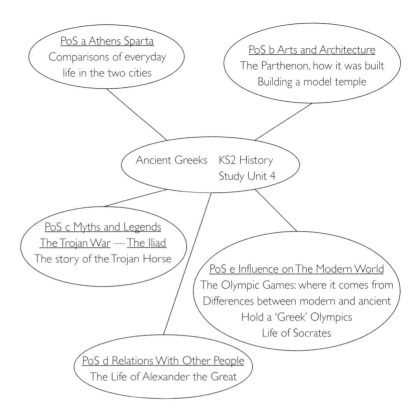

not clear on the plan, had the plan looked like the second plan (see Figure 5.2), at the outset, the failure to include Athens and Sparta could have been avoided.

Looking at the second plan, you can see that the areas that the teachers had wanted to cover are all included, except for the section on Modern Greece, and that the extra work on Athens and Sparta has been included. At a glance, the subject manager can see that all five areas of the study unit are being covered in some way, and that staff have paid due respect to the requirements of the National Curriculum. However, the plan is still far from complete, because a crucial part of the teaching of history is still missing from the plan, the Key Elements.

Key Elements are exactly that, *Key* elements, and as such, they need to be included within the medium term planning. Just as there needs to be coverage of the study units in the long term planning, and the Programmes of Study within those units in the medium term, there must also be coverage of the Key Elements. This can be achieved in several different ways.

One way is to ask all the year groups to cover all the Key Elements in their history work. This requires each year group to plan to include areas of study which can be used to show elements such as chronology, enquiry and interpretation. This places a responsibility on the class teacher which may, simply, be unworkable. As you saw in the previous chapter, when a school planned, not from the study units but from the Key Elements themselves, the unit that they were studying from provided no opportunity to look at the element of interpretations of history. Unless some work could be artificially manufactured, or the documents and source material could be discovered, then this Key Element would remain unstudied in one unit. This would create problems if, within a scheme of work for example, a subject manager had written that each year group covers all the Key Elements while studying their particular area of the history curriculum, because plainly, this would not be the case.

A far more workable approach would be to apportion Key Elements to various units, where they sit comfortably within the work planned. If this approach was adopted, the scheme of work would clearly identify that the Key Element regarding the interpretations of history was not being covered by the year group working on the local history study unit. Within the chapter on constructing a scheme of work we will discuss apportioning further. At this point, as a history subject manager, you need to consider which Key Elements would sit comfortably within the work required on Ancient Greece. Certainly chronology would be included, as would parts of the next Key Element, 'Range and Depth of Historical Knowledge and Understanding', especially the parts of this Key Element concerning characteristics of societies and the experiences of men and women, and describing and identifying reasons for historical events. Studying the Ancient Greeks is a perfect opportunity to identify interpretations of history and offers enormous scope for historical enquiry. Organisation and communication can also fairly easily be fitted into the unit.

Already, you should have identified a possible problem. Within this topic, there is the opportunity to use every Key Element, and that leads to the possibility of overloading teachers who are not that confident in the subject. Such an overload could result in very little history being taught, through a fear of the amount of historical skill required.

If the Key Elements have been apportioned, then it is unlikely that every element will need to be covered in depth. This is where a clear scheme of work is crucial, but also where your guidance and advice will create an environment where history can be taught well. If the medium term planning identifies Key Elements which do not need to be studied by the planners it is worth mentioning it! From the third and final plan of the Ancient Greek topic (see Figure 5.3), we can see how much more relevant to the National Curriculum the plan has become.

FIG 5.3
Ancient Greeks: medium term plan covering National Curriculum requirements

PoS a Athens and Sparta
Comparisons of everyday life in the two cities
*Key Element 2: Range + Depth of Historical Knowledge and Understanding a — characteristic features of societies, experiences of men and women
*Key Element 3: Interpretations of History — identify and give reasons for different ways in which the past is represented — The Role of Women in Greek Society

PoS b Arts and Architecture
The Parthenon, how it was built
Building a model temple
*Key Element 2b: describe + identify reasons for and results of historical events — Why was the Parthenon built? — Persian invasion.

Ancient Greeks   KS2 History
Study Unit 4

PoS c Myths and Legends
The Trojan War —The Iliad
— the Story of The Trojan Horse
*Key Element 5: Organisation and Communication C — communicate their knowledge + understanding of history in a variety of ways — newspaper of Trojan Horse story

PoS e Influence on The Modern World
The Olympic Games: Where it comes from
Differences between modern and ancient
Hold a 'Greek' Olympics
Life of Socrates
*Key Element 4: Historical Enquiry a — how to find out about aspects of the period studied from a range of sources — Research — what our Greek Olympics should be like, what events, who competes, what do you win?

PoS d Relations with Other People
The Life of Alexander the Great
*Key Element 5c — structured narrative of the campaigns of Alexander the Great

Also, more importantly, the plan, when placed alongside the plans from other groups, will clearly identify complete coverage of the National Curriculum, including both the Study Units and the Key Elements. Not only does this satisfy the statutory requirements of the document, it will satisfy an OFSTED inspection, when they study the school's medium term planning.

As history subject manager, planning similar to that shown in Figure 5.3 is your ultimate objective. It clearly shows what areas of the National Curriculum are being studied, and which skills are being utilised. It also demonstrates the flexibility of the document, and the ability of teachers to bend the document in directions where they wish to go. Despite the medium term planning now being tied tightly to the National Curriculum document, the teachers are still teaching the areas that they wished to cover at the start of the planning process, only perhaps they are now more focused.

For example, when covering the Key Elements, suggested activities have been included, such as a newspaper of the Trojan horse story. Teachers do appreciate this level of support, especially in a subject which they may lack confidence in. They are aware from their planning that they need to cover the story of the Trojan horse and then present the children with an opportunity to prepare a newspaper which tells the story. If they do this, they are fulfilling the requirements of the National Curriculum, which is not only their statutory obligation as teachers, it is also what all teachers want to do. What they need is guidance on how to do it, and by the assisting in the production of a planning document like Figure 5.3, you will be providing that guidance.

What you cannot, and must not, do is to provide the year groups throughout your school with a plan drawn up by yourself. As you can see, from the first sketchy outline plan with no reference to the National Curriculum, through to the final planning sheet, complete with Programmes of Study and Key Elements, the one thing we tried to keep constant was the actual content of the topic. We assumed that the teachers involved wanted to teach the areas which they highlighted on their first plan, and if teachers identify that they would like to teach areas of history, then they probably feel most confident with those areas. While Figure 5.1 was unacceptable as a planning document from the point of ensuring coverage of the National Curriculum, as an ideas sheet it is a worthwhile document.

It is from this that you could set to work. Perhaps a year group at a time, over a period of time, you could help the teachers in your school to turn their ideas into tightly planned documents which will build into a scheme of work. The key point here is to take your time. There is no rush even if OFSTED are arriving next term. As long as you have begun the process of linking planning to the National Curriculum, with a view to forming a scheme of work, there is no problem. There are two types of school which need to worry about an OFSTED inspection. The first is the school which has made very little attempt to integrate the National Curriculum planning, which is, thankfully, rare. Second is the school which shows OFSTED pristine policies and schemes of work, which, they state proudly, have been in place for a number of years, and then face the unenviable prospect of discovering that no teacher has a clue they existed, and certainly are not working from them — a fact which OFSTED would uncover very quickly. These schools are all too common. The schemes of work may have been produced at a time when they were a close match of what was being taught, but are no longer. Even worse, they could be schemes of work imposed on the staff by a subject manager. These are the schemes of work which generally never get off the ground in schools. It may seem very easy to sit down during a half term and write about what history you want everyone to cover. Take care and do not waste your time. If you have not consulted closely with staff, there is a fair chance that your scheme will end up in the cupboard gathering dust.

Consultation takes time, but it is the very best way forward, to ensure effective history throughout the school. As it takes time, disregard any attempt to rush the process, no matter what the reason. As long as you know what it is you wish to have in place at the end of the process, there will be no problems. The chapter on creating schemes of work will cover the process in more depth.

At this point, you should have assisted in producing a medium term planning sheet which clearly identifies Programmes of Study and Key Elements (for an examplar, see p. 65). Such medium term planning negates the need for complex short term planning. As the medium term planning shows coverage, all that the short term planning, be it daily or weekly, needs to show is which area of the topic you are covering at that time. References to the National Curriculum are at medium term level. The one thing missing in all this is the need for learning objectives and, from the learning objectives, the assessment which is required, if any, during this topic.

The learning objectives do not need to be exhaustive, nor do they need to be purely content based. They should show clearly what the teacher expects the children to learn, which will tie in with schemes of work, and the progression of historical skills through the school. Again you should be able to advise teachers as to sensible learning objectives, rather than telling them what they should be doing. For example, having helped a year group mould their ideas sheet on the Ancient Greeks into a fully fledged National Curriculum planning document, how would you respond if the members of the year group wrote the following as learning objectives for the topic.

1 Children should be able to compare life in Athens and Sparta
2 Children can show an understanding of the ancient Olympics
3 Children can retell the story of the Trojan horse

Hopefully, you would be positive, before pointing the teachers in the direction of what they have already written. The learning objectives for the topic are already on the planning sheet! For example — a learning objective when studying the Olympic games could be that children show that they are able to use sources such as pots to identify different aspects of the games, maybe the sports involved. The inclusion of Key Elements, and the writing tasks underneath them shows the teachers what the learning objective should be. Children should be able to say why the Parthenon was built and they should be able to write a structured narrative of Alexander's campaigns. The objectives are there already, teachers do not have to invent them and they are, even more importantly, very closely tied to both the National Curriculum and the work being done. Perhaps, to cover the recall of historical information, a short end of term test could be added, containing questions on what has been learnt. Otherwise the work children undertake within the course of the topic are the learning objectives, and the children's ability to carry out the tasks mentioned on the plan will show whether or not they have achieved the learning objectives.

If assessment is needed, it, too, is contained within the work required to cover the Key Elements. For example, PoS a: Athens and Sparta, contains a Key Element which calls for the study of the role of women. Within the Level Descriptions, Level 4 states that children show how some aspects of the past have been represented and interpreted in different ways. An assessment of this, perhaps, if it was agreed upon by the staff, within this topic, would be for children to offer two different women's stories — one telling the traditionally accepted narrative of Greek women as staying at home, doing as the male Greeks told them, and one telling the story of a Greek woman doing just about everything in society men did. There are plenty of sources to support both stories, and no historian is entirely sure of the role of women in Ancient Greece. The child's ability to produce this dual piece of work confirms that they are at Level 4, hey presto, assessment complete! (See the chapter on assessment strategies for advice on creating manageable assessments in history.)

As you can see, the benefits of high quality medium term planning are multitudinous, and it is the role of the coordinator to ensure that such quality exists. It does not take much more time, after the initial ideas have come to mind, to tie the ideas to the Programmes of Study and the Key Elements, and once it is done for the first time, it takes very little time to repeat the exercise when the topic comes to be taught again. You will find that teachers grow in confidence when they realise that it does not take too much to bend what they want to teach into a clearly recognisable topic offering coverage of the National Curriculum. Repetition of the topic offers scope to expand areas that worked particularly well and

FIG 5.4
History topic evaluation

TOPIC: Ancient Greece
STUDY UNIT: 4

PoS a — comparisons of Athens + Sparta went well. Role of Women was hampered by few resources available.

PoS b — excellent. Used photos to design our models. Children able to say, in most cases, why Parthenon was built.

PoS c — good. Need more time to produce newspapers.

PoS d — very few of the children could produce a structured narrative of any quality.

PoS e — excellent. Thoroughly enjoyable 'Olympics'. Perhaps need a couple of discuses in school. (We borrowed from local secondary school).

Overall — Very enjoyable topic, which children were very interested in. Perhaps need a little more time?

re-evaluate those areas which did not go as well as expected. Here lies another way to raise the standard of history in the school. At the end of a history topic, why not send a teacher a copy of their plan, asking them to highlight the areas that they covered, so monitoring the coverage of the National Curriculum? It is painless, quick and an easy way for you to check on what is being taught in the subject within the school. You could also ask the teacher to evaluate the areas of the topic covered. This does not need to take forever, it could amount to a few words on each area. Below is an example of an evaluation on the Ancient Greece topic that we have built on throughout this chapter (see Figure 5.4).

There are several areas of importance to note in this evaluation. First, the overall comment should raise a smile. 'An enjoyable topic' is a topic which is taught well. The more enjoyable it is the more enthusiastic the teacher is, and the more enthusiastic the children are. We would direct a 'pat on the back' towards this year group, and say encouraging things about the quality of the teaching, to build on the obvious enthusiasm and create a confidence which will help the teachers when the topic comes back, as well as raise the year group's self-esteem.

Second, the need for more time is a common problem. It can be addressed by spreading the topic out more, perhaps by having it run into another topic, or by trimming the amount of work down a little. For example, on the medium term plan, the life of Socrates is mentioned — this may well be surplus to requirements so can be left out. It has not been mentioned on the evaluation, and a quick check of the highlighted plan, will show whether it was taught or not. Then, there is a need to allocate resources for a specific identified problem. The year group has said that its teaching of the role of women, a critical area of the Key Elements, was hampered by a lack of resources. You should take note, and begin to look for resources such as photos, books and facsimiles of Greek pottery to help in this area.

Perhaps, most crucially of all, the fact that most of the children found it difficult to produce a structured narrative of any quality is an issue of major importance. It is an area which has been defined as a Key Element in the National Curriculum, and if children are failing to fulfil this requirement then you would need to look closely at the reasons why. Perhaps this is the first time structured narrative has been a Key Element in the history planning of these children, and they will re-visit this area again. If this is the case then the children need to be monitored to ensure that they progress, and the next teacher to cover that specific Key Element needs to be aware of the children's need for support in this area.

If this is not the case, and the children have already covered the structured narrative area part of the Key Elements, then you need to look again at the teaching methods for this particular area, and this will, of course, have been made easy. After all, you will have the history plans for each year group, identifying where this Key Element had been taught before.

By identifying areas of weakness or poor performance in such a manner, you can target resources and skills at these areas. For example, you may find it necessary to increase the number of times that structured narratives are formally covered. You may decide to find resources such as history texts that present events as stories so that the children become more aware of longer pieces of historical writing. Before a problem of this nature can be tackled successfully, it is important that the problem is identified and acknowledged. By introducing the evaluation, which will take your colleagues only a few moments to complete, you are providing an opportunity to identify such areas. To acknowledge them as a problem, which the evaluating teacher has, requires your input as well.

For example, what if the comment had come from a teacher of Year 3 children — perhaps the expectations of the children's work were far too high. Perhaps the topic has not included structured narratives in the past, so the teachers have been approaching this Key Element for the first time, and they may need some guidance. Perhaps the appearance of the comment confirms comments from other teachers about the same Key Element. Whichever way it is taken the evaluation provides a critical line of communication between yourself as a coordinator and your colleagues. If they communicate success, praise them if they communicate potential problems, try to deal with them. Communication is the key in the whole planning process — use it wisely and it can unlock the door to increased standards of attainment in the subject.

Monitoring planned and taught history

The first thing to monitor is current history within your school. The KS2 planning documents included, should help you to see what history is being taught where. When you have started to create your school specific Scheme of Work, then your system of monitoring should resemble what we discuss below.

No matter how carefully planned and thoroughly linked with the National Curriculum it is, no matter how well resourced and well advised teachers are, the plan can still be, at worst, ignored, or, with the best intentions, trimmed.

Trimming is often a necessary fact of life for the modern primary school teacher. With too much to teach and too little time to do it in, it tempts even the most virtuous teacher. We have all thought it — and all done it. Something on the medium term plan is missed out or marginalised because you must practise the assembly, you must sort out sports day, you

---

Methods of monitoring
- Highlighted planning sheet
- Evaluation sheet
- Displays
- Children's work
- Children themselves

must go on a trip, etc. This can, however, create havoc. If you sit in an OFSTED interview, and tell the history inspector how certain you are that Year 2 covers each of the three strands of the study unit, only to find out that the famous lives that they should have studied were missed out because of the nativity play, then you will not have done yourself any favours. It is not enough to merely set up the schemes of work, and monitor the medium term planning to ensure coverage on paper. The paper coverage must become real coverage, actual lessons, with real time spent on the identified Key Elements. While the evaluation sheets mentioned above will help you to see what history is being taught, there needs to be time spent in other ways to monitor the subject.

One obvious way, at first glance, is to look at the books of children being taught history. Borrowing a child's book from a class and checking through it can help you to see what has been taught. If you keep the medium term plan next to you as you go through the child's book, just tick off those areas you can see have been covered. In some schools this is the only form of monitoring used and this can create problems.

Some areas of the history curriculum lend themselves to the written word, or even the drawn picture, but some definitely do not. For example, if a class decides to produce a Shakespearean play while studying the Tudors to write about what happened during the course of this would be an English exercise as opposed to a historical one, and frankly a waste of valuable time. The play itself, the production of it and attempts at Tudor authenticity should be the objectives of such an exercise. There has been too much emphasis on children writing down everything they have done, and in some cases it is too much. One school staff we know has found a way around the impasse. They take photographs and display them. It sounds so simple, but so many schools have either time-costly stories or no evidence of the event at all. Photographs on display provide the perfect answer. They record the event, they take up no extra classroom time and yet they offer evidence of the coverage of an area of the curriculum. There is no need for written evidence, and therefore no need to waste long periods of time asking the children to write reports that are not specific learning objectives.

Some teachers that we are aware of try to have at least one display in the classroom based on photographic evidence. One of the best ideas for displaying photographs on a long term basis was seen in a classroom, where a class 'notice board' included photos of several different activities, ranging from science trips to music work shops, all labelled and dated. The teacher had stated that she thought that writing a narrative on the events of the trip was unnecessary, when the photos showed everyone who came into the classroom exactly when and where they had been, and some of the things that they had done when they got there. The obvious usefulness of photographs, to return to our example plan of the Ancient Greeks Study Unit, is the Olympic games. The Key Element covered by this area is about historical enquiry and not report writing so teachers should be able to concentrate on this aspect. When the children hold their Olympics it will be the culmination of this research, not the beginning of a piece of work entitled 'What We Did'. The only evidence needed to show that the event took place are a few photos on the wall.

This saves time and makes it more possible to cover the rest of the history on the plan properly, and it is coverage and quality, after all, that you are concerned with. The more time available the better the subject can be dealt with.

Photographs, the children's work and the evaluation sheet make valuable evidence for you when monitoring the implementation of history in your school. You can also glean evidence from displays either in the classroom or around the school, of what is being covered. It may be worth pushing colleagues to have a history display somewhere in their classroom, illustrating some work covered. Many teachers already display such work, but others will need a helping hand. Suggestions, such as including photos of artefacts (if not artefacts themselves) and posters, would be appreciated by colleagues who, perhaps, wonder whether a history display is of any use.

Another valuable source of information is the children themselves. When OFSTED inspection teams arrive in schools, they will spend a considerable amount of time talking to children about the work that they have done, what they enjoyed about it and how it was taught. The OFSTED process recognises that the child, who is, after all, why we are in education, is the important factor of any teaching in any school. Why then are schools being too slow to pick this up? If you wish to find out how well a topic has been taught, ask a child. A five minute chat with one or two children, asking them what they have done, what they have enjoyed and what they have disliked will provide you with a mine of information. If the children are very young, use their books or displays as prompts asking them questions about them. Older children will not need the prompts as long as your questions are focused. For example, don't expect a full response from a question like 'What have you liked most in history?'. This question normally gives way to plenty of 'Umming' and 'Erring' before the inevitable shrug of the shoulders. A much better question would be, 'I hear your class competed in an Olympics of your own, that sounds like fun. What events were you in?'

This will provide you with a way in to discussing how the children found out what events should be in an ancient Olympics, so examining the coverage of Key Element 4 — Historical Enquiry, which is on the medium term plan. Children are hugely under-used sources of information in schools and, in our opinion, an absolutely vital part of monitoring the provision of history within your school. OFSTED will ask them, not because of any devious attempt to trip teachers up, but because a child should be able to tell them exactly what they have done in each subject, especially when the school (in other words, the class teacher and you as the history subject manager) has drawn up carefully planned learning objectives for the children concerned. It seems the obvious way to evaluate the success of a particular learning objective, to ask those who are supposed to have learnt, but very few schools ask the children. To us, and hopefully now to you too, the child will become an integral part of your monitoring process.

What, then, happens when you realise, as subject manager, that what is planned is not what is taught? Do not confront the teacher, demanding to know why a Programme of Study has not been studied. That will achieve nothing, except create acrimony and resentment. You will have to talk to the teacher but as an adviser not as a dictator. It may well be that the study unit was over planned and simply had too much content to be covered in the time available. If this is the case, then next time the study unit is taught, the teacher should be able to plan more realistically. No matter what the reason for your colleague not covering an area, you can pretty much guarantee it will not be for lack of trying. If your schemes of work are in place and the Key Elements are properly apportioned, then whichever Key Element has not been covered will be covered again, or has been covered before. They will miss out, perhaps, on a stage of progression, but the cause is not hopeless. Just because the time for covering a study unit has elapsed, does not mean that that history cannot be covered again. One school of which we are aware studies the Egyptians before Christmas, and has an Egyptian 'Feast Day' just before Easter, so that the children are reminded of the topic and experience it again. The school in question thus uses the Feast Day as a revision aid, and as such it is considered very useful.

If the Key Element cannot be covered at a different time during the academic year then so be it. These things do happen and, in a realistic world, we just have to accept it and get on with it. It would then become your responsibility, as subject manager, to inform the next teacher to cover that Key Element as the children have not experienced it during their previous topic.

Part three

Whole school policies and schemes of work

Chapter 6
Developing a history policy

Chapter 7
Developing a scheme of work

It is a fact that the existence of subject policy documents and schemes of work for every area of the curriculum in all state-funded primary schools has not yet been achieved. Some areas are more neglected than others and this is evidenced through no, or out-of-date, documentation. History, being a relatively new subject in primary schools, needs to be developed through a carefully thought out policy statement which should be a distillation of the current practice in the school. This section will deal with the general and overarching considerations you, as subject manager will need to apprise the staff of, as well as the practical considerations of translating policy to practice.

The policy document must be linked to the school development plan and will then provide a focus for everyone involved in the school's curriculum.

Chapter 6 — Developing a history policy

Developing a policy for history might be thought to be the most challenging of tasks. It is, in some respects, but is also thought-provoking and exciting. If the focus is to translate existing practice into a policy statement then there is a good deal of work to be done in setting it down on paper in a brief, but understandable, way. It is even harder to begin with a blank sheet of paper and try to develop a policy document in a vacuum. The point of developing a whole school policy is that it is owned by the staff, describes what is actually happening in everybody's classroom and gives some indication of the direction the school is going with regard to your area. School policy documentation varies from school to school. Commonly, there is a short statement of policy, one or two sides of A4, followed or accompanied by a file which contains the detail in the form of a scheme of work. The format for developing a history policy detailed below is that described by Mike Harrison (1995) and is a useful structure to use with the staff. It can then be altered in line with their views, if necessary.

A whole school policy can:
- publicly demonstrate the school's intentions in history;
- help make a case for funding;
- give information to governors, parents and inspectors;
- provide a framework for planning;
- aid coherence, continuity, progression and shape priorities, and;
- assist in achieving uniformity and consistency in school decision making.

If there is an existing history policy statement then this should always be the starting point for the development of a policy that reflects present day considerations. In order to evaluate the present policy statement, it is useful to have a focused set of questions to ask of it as you read. Below are some to help you in this. As you read the policy, ask yourself firstly, does the document satisfy any or all of the purposes listed. Secondly, ask could it be made to do so. Thirdly, note any omissions which will need to be addressed in the new policy.

Does the policy statement:
- help focus the mind of various decision making groups toward common aims;
- improve the effectiveness of meetings by helping us all broadly to share each other's understanding of the situation;
- help participants understand teaching and learning strategies employed by other staff;
- help create a team spirit in making public the school's goals;
- offer a means of evaluation;
- help clarify functions and responsibilities of staff, and;
- aid new staff by providing a supportive framework to help them to settle in.

The seven sections of the prototype policy presented here are offered to give you a skeleton on which to hang your own ideas and suggestions. Most areas will need discussion and agreement with staff to be meaningful but it is sometimes useful to have a starting document if only to focus discussion.

Introduction/rationale

You should always start with a general statement of the school's agreed intent in history, which is suitable for teachers, school governors, the LEA and OFSTED inspectors. The rationale sets up expectations about the way the knowledge and skill of history are to be taught so it is important that it is well-discussed. It is a truism, which needs to be reiterated to all staff when drawing up a policy statement, that every school is unique. This is the result of the fact that every school operates on a particular set of beliefs which is the outcome of the mixture of the school community (headteachers, teachers, support staff, children, parents etc.), the LEA and the influences of society at large. The rationale/introduction should recognise that the children, in your school, have specific and general needs related to their own community and society in general. This leads on naturally for the learning goals to be established on these basic needs and beliefs. These goals, needs and beliefs are formulated into a set of aims for the future of the children and the school.

Aims

The aims section of the policy will follow on from the opening, general statement which needs to be based on National Curriculum requirements and to declare that every child should have access to learning in history and that the school is dedicated to achievement in this area. The statement should also reflect the school's ethos and overall aims. As we have said, this vital opening section expresses the philosophy of the school and, as such, must be drawn up jointly by the headteacher and you and agreed by staff and governors before detailed work on guidelines can begin in earnest. Once it is agreed, it will colour the whole document.

We have discussed in Parts 1 and 2 the importance of a shared understanding of the nature of history both as the story of the past and the study of the past. The degree of agreement among the staff about what history is to be taught and how will be in evidence in the way that the aims are written. The order in which they are present will also indicate importance in hierarchical terms unless it is specifically stated that all the aims are of equal importance. You, as subject manager, must lead discussion on this vital first section and then write and re-write the aims until a consensus on the wording is achieved. Below are some examples of aims which might help start staff discussion (though be wary of using them from the beginning in case they close down the possibility of other aims getting an airing).

The aims of the history teaching in our school are:
- to develop the acquisition of knowledge which provides insight into the cultural heritage of the local, national and international community;
- to develop an understanding of the present through a study of the past;

- to develop an understanding of past events and issues from the perspective of people who lived in those times;
- to develop an intrinsic interest in history;
- to give children a sense of personal identity through the study of the past;
- to develop an appreciation of the social, economic, political, cultural and aesthetic dimensions of history;
- to develop the key concepts of time/chronology; cause/effect; continuity/change and similarity/difference;
- to develop a critical and reflective attitude to words as sources of evidence.

Below this statement of aims, there should be a description of who has prepared the present policy and when, and who the subject manager is (this may be one and the same person, of course).

Implementation

Experiences you intend, as a school, to give children throughout the age range in order to achieve the above aims should appear here. This may take the form of an interpretation of the National Curriculum Programmes of Study and Attainment Targets which take account of the circumstances of your school. This section is not the scheme of work but the document does require sufficient detail to ensure continuity of approach and progression of work throughout the school.

There is also a place for helping to gain agreement in the methods which will be used to promote learning in history. If this can be done, it may be recorded at this point in your policy document and this will help to remind everyone on what they agreed

Example
The delivery of history will be through an integrated Programme of Study in accordance with the requirements of the National Curriculum. In KS1 this will mostly take the form of topic/thematic work. At KS2 the children will be taught history as a separate subject in its own right. Children will work individually, in groups and as a whole class in history as is considered appropriate by the teacher.

Do not forget to include an equal opportunities statement and any history specific multicultural issues. For example:

> All children regardless of race, gender, physical ability . . . will be given equal access to history.

In history, classroom management will take account of such issues, and classroom materials free from bias will be actively sought.

The names and roles of persons responsible for overseeing or managing the implementation of this policy need to be recorded here along with the various responsibilities of head and classteachers with regard to it.

Finally, include methods for monitoring the implementation of this policy. Who is responsible for seeing that the agreed practices are being carried out in all classes? Who is to ensure children's entitlement? It may be covered above but still might need to be stated here. How will this be done? The policy will need to be reviewed to maintain its relevance to the school as it moves forward. It is useful to set a date for its formal review by the staff as soon as it is completed. In this way it becomes part of the ongoing curriculum review and accepted as such. A sudden realisation that history has been left out of the cycle could mean a rushed, ill-considered attempt at revision.

Chapter 7

Developing a scheme of work

The scheme of work is the document which shows how the policy is translated into practice. As such, it is much lengthier and more detailed than the policy statement. The list of what might be appropriate to include is appended below with some examples of what to include.

Scheme of work

I Timing of the history study units

This will give the timetable for the teaching of the units from Year 1 to Year 6. This will ensure that each child will have all the history content that s/he is entitled to have. This is not as easy a task as it appears. You will have to ensure that any classes that are mixed in age are carefully catered for, or some may miss out a unit or repeat one. However, with the advent of the National Curriculum, the focus of the majority of primary schools is on collaborative planning. The time of the autonomous teacher working in splendid isolation has passed. Your role, as subject manager, is made easier by this philosophical shift. The staff, led by you, will negotiate and agree on a structure for the delivery of the units with ease.

2 Historical skills and concepts

This list will not be long but its inclusion here is vital to underline the point that giving the children the tools of the historian's trade is to be done as an integral part of the history syllabus and from Year 1 to Year 6. Suggestions for their development might usefully be included here, too.

3 Teaching styles

The place for didactic and exploratory teaching will be placed here with examples of each. The use of the variety of classroom groupings will also be catalogued and illustrated.

4 Resources

This will catalogue the equipment available, and centrally housed, to which all teachers will need access at certain times in their history topics. In addition, the resources particular to each classroom will be listed so that the spread of resources can be scrutinised by all staff. This is a useful professional development ploy. When a teacher notices someone making use of something they have not got, it makes them think about their practice. The issue of resources is dealt with in more detail later in the chapter, and links with health and safety are considered.

5 Children's work

Here would be placed the practice of the school which would ensure the KS1 children could communicate their awareness and understanding of history in a variety of ways. The written story narrative should not be the sole or dominant method for young children to reveal their learning in history, as you and the staff know. It does no harm to list the variety of ways — it will be useful for the supply teacher as well as an aide memoire for staff at the planning sessions to keep in mind. This is equally true of KS2 children when they show what they know about history.

6 Progression and continuity

Progression through the key stages should be clearly signalled in the planning of the units. Here it will be appropriate to emphasise that 1 and 2 above are the starting point for these considerations. These will be enhanced and developed through the ongoing moderation that is built into the school development plan. Any practical outcomes associated with moderation meetings, and accepted by staff, should be put here.

7 Differentiation

Differentiation is easily thrown away in an overview statement but the initiation, monitoring and updating of differentiated work programmes to match pupils' needs and progress them will tax the skills and time allocation of even the most effective subject manager (Boyle, 1995, p. 119). Even with this warning, it is necessary to try to deal with the issue here. After all, 'the best guidelines indicated how differentiation could be achieved in each unit of work' (Lloyd, 1994) — the ways in which this is to be achieved should be recorded here. The basic statement that reading attainment is taken into account when written sources or text-related information are used is essential, but the far more difficult task of describing differentiation, in historical terms, is a nettle to be grasped. The best way to do this is to scrutinise the teachers' planning for each unit looking for differentiation. These examples could then be given in the scheme of work to help others in their planning for differentiation.

8 Record keeping and assessment

This is the place for an effective means of interpreting achievement and the ways that history achievements are recorded and assessed in the school at present will be itemised and exemplified here (see Part 3). You will have led (or planned for) a review of this aspect and a statement that this is constantly under review will encourage staff to evaluate critically each assessment done for its usefulness in the learning needs of the child.

9 Provision for special needs

The Common Requirements state that the Programmes of Study for each key stage should be taught to the great majority of pupils in the key stage, in ways appropriate to their abilities. This places the onus on you, as subject manager, to make available materials suitable for wide attainment ranges and to support the staff in their teaching in history from this point of view. Your expertise and knowledge of what materials are available will be at a premium when dealing with the small number (according to the NC history document) of pupils who may need the provision of resources selected from earlier or later key stages. It is necessary to record here that colleagues will liaise with the subject manager and the special needs coordinator to discuss individual needs in this area. This enables the classroom teacher to see a clear path to some practical help if she gets into difficulty. The general statements about appropriate provision being made available for pupils who need to use means of communication other than speech, non-sighted methods of reading, non-visual or non-aural ways of acquiring information, technological aids in practical and written work or aids or adapted equipment to allow access to practical activities within and beyond school must be made history subject specific.

10 Cross-curricular themes and dimensions

In this section there will be reference to the ways these are taught throughout the school with particular reference to history. However, there will be an important liaising role for you here to ensure that there is a spread of these themes and dimensions across the units and year groups. The children will be encouraged to deal with the concept of equality issues in every area of history but the emphasis on, for example, health education might have more importance in one unit than another. It is up to you to lead discussion to develop a strategy for the timing and emphasis of these aspects in history.

11 Multicultural education

This is a fundamentally important aspect of children's entitlement in history. We have discussed this earlier but here there should be an emphasis on how each unit will access this area for children.

12 Information Technology

As it is a requirement that pupils should be given opportunities to develop and apply their IT capability in their study of history, reference should be made to the inclusion of IT in the planning of each unit. Examples of its successful integration should be put here.

13 Health and safety

The history resources will be scrutinised in the light of the school's health and safety policy. Any materials that may be considered unsafe for some children's use should be listed along with a reminder of the responsibility of all to staff to monitor the wear and tear on equipment and to report any concerns. This should be followed by a statement of when and by whom there will be a regular survey of history resources from the health and safety angle.

A look ahead to history in Year 7

Finally, a synopsis of the history work covered in the first year of secondary education might usefully be appended here.

Assessment and recording of pupils' progress

This aspect has been dealt with earlier, but this is the point at which you should list the purposes of assessment. Include agreed methods of record keeping and times at which such assessments are made. The key to this section is minimalism as there are ten subjects, plus RE, in the curriculum and the demands on teachers should not be excessive. Items for inclusion here might include:

- Teachers' records of children's experiences are those kept in annotated forecast books — or on a medium term planning sheet;
- A sample of children's work in history, which demonstrates their abilities in the subject, is selected and saved, possibly in a Record of Achievement folder;
- The assessment summary sheet, which can be as brief as a photocopy of the Level Descriptions, highlighting the level achieved by the vast majority of the children, and annotating those children who did not reach that level, or who exceeded it, will also need to follow the child through their school lives.

This section should not be at variance with the school's assessment and recording and reporting policy. It should state, how, what, where and how often. It might even say why records are kept, what the real purpose of plotting pupils' progress in history is in your school.

How do you report progress to parents? It will be useful here to give guidance to the staff about what to look for as an indication of what is meant by progression. A commonly agreed statement like the one below may help.

Example:
As children progress they should be able to gain more of an understanding of the world around them and their place in it. They should comprehend the need for evidence to support assertions, and be able to demonstrate their skills at finding and presenting such evidence. It is the job of your school to ensure, to the best ability of the staff in it, that children have a chance to progress towards a better understanding of their place in the world, their past and, their role in society. George Orwell was not overstating matters when he declared that those who control the past, control the present. It is crucial that children gain an understanding of the past and acquire the skills of historians.

Resources

This is where you include a comprehensive list of equipment (with serial numbers if appropriate), books in the library to support history teaching and learning, software, videos, working models etc. available for teachers to use. Your policy should indicate who gets to use what, when and how, where they are stored, and any security features to help in the efficient deployment of resources.

A look ahead to future purchasing in history is helpful — you might want to put in a statement here regarding future resource development, for example:
■ The school development plan sets out an objective of further acquisitions of artefacts to support the Key Stage 2 history unit dealing with Life Since the 1930s over the next two years.

- The software to support the Non-European Study Unit will be enhanced as a matter of urgency.

The school development plan is a useful tool to ensure that resources and time are allocated carefully. Most schools operate a rolling development cycle, where the foundation subjects such as history, will appear every few years. When the subject appears it gains a spending priority and provides a subject manager with some muscle when it comes to acquiring resources. One of the key features of your behaviour at this stage is to be bold. If you do not request items you will not get them. If you do request them, but financial constraints result in their not being purchased, you can always go back at the start of the next financial year and request again. When history is on the development plan, you should be able, through your monitoring of the subject, to target specific areas quite accurately so ensuring that colleagues have the resources they need. If a purchasing plan exists in any detail, for example, where a school is starting from scratch with the purchasing of artefacts, then it would make a useful appendix to your policy document.

Health and Safety

There should be a section on health and safety — either as a separate issue or appended to the resource section. As with all areas of teaching, the safety of the children must be paramount. History may not seem like a physically dangerous subject, but the thought of some children handling a Victorian mincer will make any teacher wince. It is perhaps useful to include a set of handling rules — to be included in the appendix. They could include such basic points as:
- always handle an artefact with both hands;
- only handle an artefact when told to do so, and;
- only one person should handle an artefact at a time.

These may seem like common sense, but we have seen these basic considerations flouted. If any materials are required for projects which stem from the history study units, they must be safe for all to use. An attempt to add texture to a Tudor style portrait by adding wallpaper paste to the paint could well be visually stunning, but if the paste contains fungicide, it could also make the children itch. A list of safe materials, usually those from main educational suppliers, should be provided so that your colleagues can be sure. In addition, it is crucial to include repair arrangements for equipment (with telephone numbers and necessary forms).

Staff development

The successful implementation of the policy will require INSET, both school based and using outside agencies. The policy document will appear more complete and credible if such arrangements are included here.

Staff development can occur, of course, in a number of ways, either at an individual level or as a whole school. Identifying the needs of the staff through study unit evaluation sheets should help to focus INSET. When you become aware of courses, make sure your colleagues are also aware. For example, we know one history subject manager who does not attend history content based INSET courses provided by the LEA, but who ensures that her colleagues do, when they return from the course, she asks them for the ideas they have picked up. She responds positively and enthusiastically and so succeeds in raising the confidence level of staff around her as a result.

Your school-based INSET time will be very limited, and probably decided by the subject's position within the school development plan. Again, to use it effectively, you will need to be aware of the relative strengths and weaknesses of your colleagues, and focus your INSET on raising both the confidence and the competence level of your colleagues. You cannot do that if you do not know what level they are at. This is where the monitoring and evaluating of the subject becomes crucial. If the staff are to develop, they have to know that they need to develop. This is a task requiring great diplomacy. Finally, be focused, aiming especially at areas where either you yourself, or your colleagues, or inspectors have identified weaknesses in teaching.

Review of this policy

The headteacher and staff will need to review this policy
to take account of changing circumstances. The date for its
reconsideration may be stated in this final section. You might
consider discussing with staff the inclusion of measures by
which the success of the policy and its implementation may
be judged. These may include teachers' and children's
perceptions: children's work and any other written evidence,
a review of teachers' forecasts, parents' and governors'
responses or classroom observations.

Developing a scheme of work: an example

The development of a school specific scheme of work sounds
such an overwhelming task that many teachers simply do not
know where to start. Their response to this feeling of dread is
to write down anything regardless of whether or not it mirrors
actual practice within the school. This makes the scheme
of work a useless document, as it simply fails to address
reality. Where, then, can you start with what is, and must
be understood as, a mammoth task? The first thing you can
do is draw up a timetable, realistically based on what you
can achieve. There is no rush where such development is
concerned, and we have generally found that the schemes of
work that have been written in a hurry are the ones that fail to
supply the support that they should. It will take time for you
to collect together the things you will need — medium term
planning, children's work and colleagues' evaluations. If the
scheme of work is to be successful it must reflect what is
actually being done in your school. Therefore, you need to find
out what is being done, and use this as your starting point.

If your medium term planning is as detailed as it should be
(see Part 2), you should be able to ensure coverage of the
National Curriculum quite easily. The difficult part will be
ensuring that the Key Elements are covered sufficiently. These
are examplars which would demonstrate coverage of content
and Key Elements fairly easily across Key Stage 2. It is up to
you to decide which elements are the most important — each

school has different priorities. These elements should be covered at some stage in almost all, if not all, of the study units. For example, you may decide that every teacher must cover the Historical Enquiry Key Element, so you need to ensure that they do. How can you manage this? Most teachers will cover, some unwittingly, almost all the Key Elements at some stage in their history teaching. What you need to find amidst the medium term planning and the children's work, and your monitoring of the subject, is **how** they cover them. Then you need to formalise this coverage, just as we did with our planning sheets for the Ancient Greek topic in Part 2. That way you can be certain that the whole National Curriculum is covered.

Your scheme of work should be a document that a new teacher could pick up in the staffroom and know exactly what they were teaching. One way that we have seen for a scheme of work to be built up is for the teachers to make copies of worksheets or lesson plans that they do, so that their work builds into a sort of central file, which they can follow when next covering that topic. Their work in the file is translated by the subject manager into National Curriculum Key Elements or Programmes of Study, and also linked with the Level Descriptions, so that the teachers are aware of the level that they are teaching at. This aids progression enormously and fairly easily. A teacher can see from her scheme of work that a child attempting a certain task may be working at a level much lower or higher than their current abilities.

Another way that we have seen a scheme of work developed, and a method that can be adapted to any subject, involves INSET or staff meeting times, but can be very profitable. Before the meeting, the subject manager would have photocopied the Programme of Study for each unit, and the Key Elements that they wished each year group to cover. Each year group teacher is then given this information, and asked to fill out a piece of paper for each Programme of Study, that looks like this:

Study Unit
Programme of Study
How it is taught
Resources
Links with Key Elements

Any worksheets included in the resource list should be included with the sheet. As this method involves staff saying **how** they actually teach something, it cannot fail to mirror actual practice within your school. It may even be worth not including links with Key Elements, but adding them yourself when the sheets are completed. Most importantly, you need to prioritise — it may slow down colleagues who struggle to link practice to Key Elements, and you may feel that this is not the objective of staff meetings or INSET time. This method has produced extremely detailed schemes of work that have effectively reduced planning and preparation time because all that teachers need to do is refer to the schemes.

Whichever method you choose to build a scheme of work, remember that it needs to be done in close consultation with your colleagues. Nothing could be more soul-destroying than spending a large amount of time developing a scheme of work only to see it gather dust on the shelf. Both the methods we have described above will help your scheme of work become a document of crucial importance to the school, and of great use to your colleagues. This is what a scheme of work should be — a dynamic, living document — not a book end.

Chapter 8
How do you measure a child's historical development?

Chapter 9
Responding to children's work and report writing

This section deals with all aspects of assessment in history as well as the ways in which progression and continuity across the age groups and Key Stages can be achieved. The variety of assessment purposes and techniques are rehearsed so that you can work with the staff on them to develop a comprehensive, though uncluttered, way of measuring historical development in children. Marking of children's work is an important area for staff to have a coherent view on and this will also be explored in the history curriculum context. The skills of report writing will also be discussed as will the uses to which these can be put.

Chapter 8

How do you measure a child's historical development?

One of the most contentious issues of recent years has been the introduction of assessment, and the time consuming practices that grew up around its introduction. Since the Dearing Review, the issue of assessment has again been the subject of discussion and some consternation among teachers because of what they perceive as a singular lack of guidance from on high, especially in the foundation subjects. This has led to a variety of practice in this area. Some schools have stopped assessing in all subjects, some only assess in the core areas, and some have simply carried on assessing absolutely everything. It is a difficult area in schools, not only because of the lack of guidance, but also because of the emotions it arouses. Many teachers found the concept of assessment as it appeared in the early years of the National Curriculum quite daunting, and with good reason. In the early days, it was time consuming, ill-judged and unguided. Each school did something different, and so the records that could be passed from school to school were complicated and largely ignored. This must not be allowed to happen again. Assessment should be purposeful and useful, and help inform planning for teachers.

Measuring historical development in a child is a challenging task for the busy classroom teacher. You, as subject manager, have an important role in developing in the staff a confidence and an expertise in this area. The temptation to give a content-based test to check on the knowledge base of the child will be there. If you, as the subject manager, have encouraged the staff to see history in more complex terms than fact gathering then the measurement techniques you will adopt in looking at children's history knowledge, skills and attitudes will be more refined and diffuse than a pencil and paper test. It is important to accurately assess pupils' understanding and the way it progresses within and across specific subject areas and you will need to convince staff of this. They must always see relevance in any assessment they do, otherwise it can be regarded as a way of gathering paper for 'them', rather than for themselves and for the benefit of their children. Before we look in more detail at the ways and means of assessing children's historical knowledge and skills, it is useful to rehearse the several purposes of assessment with the staff in order to clarify matters. It is of vital importance, after all, that each assessment carried out in history has a purpose. The assessment cannot just be to fulfil the needs of the school's assessment policy — it needs to serve a useful, learning-based purpose as well.

The purposes of assessment are many and varied. They are outlined briefly below for you to use as an aide memoire with the staff. This will help ensure that all purposes are covered in the school history policy.

1   Formative assessment provides information for teachers to use in deciding 'where next?' with a child's learning and can also provide feedback to pupils about their achievements. For example, 'That's excellent work, Sean, now I think you can write sentences for the story you've sequenced'.

2   Summative assessment provides evidence of achievement. For example, 'This is the best piece of work you've done this term, Uzhair, would you like to put it in your Record of Achievement folder?'.

3   Diagnostic assessment gains an in-depth analysis of a child's learning. For example, 'Fiona's work shows that she has a very limited understanding of chronology. How can I help at this point?'.

4   Evaluative assessment helps teachers and schools to see where further effort, resources and change needs to take place. For example, 'The children don't seem to understand that concept. Perhaps I should approach it again from a different angle'.

5   Informative assessment helps communication with parents, governors and the LEA. For example, 'Charlie's time-line is excellent, you must come in and see it'.

6   Assessment also offers the chance of professional development. Teachers can discuss work in moderation meetings during which they can be offered access to new ways of thinking by you and other colleagues. For example, 'Discussing my class assessments with their teacher from last year has really helped me focus on potential problems'.

All of the assessments carried out in history need to fulfil one of these purposes. The most worthwhile purpose, from the viewpoint of the classroom teacher, is the formative assessment, as it offers the opportunity to plan the next step for the child. To carry out effective assessment in history, we need to look beyond the content of the study units, back to the Key Elements, the skills of history, the tools of the trade if you like.

The rest of this section offers a model of assessment. We stress it is only a model — a selection of some of the best ideas we have seen. It has been designed to be as quick to administer and record as possible, while still providing the information that is necessary to ensure that each child is able to progress in the subject. It also has the added advantage of making report writing easier at the end of the year, as you will see. You should critically evaluate its usefulness in the light of your school's particular circumstances and decide when and how to offer some or all of it for the staff's consideration. It is probable that some of these techniques are already being used by your colleagues. If they are, but in an individual, or idiosyncratic way then it is useful to focus on these as a starting point towards getting consensus for their inclusion in the whole school policy.

A model for assessment in history

All teachers would agree, to a greater or lesser extent that, children's knowledge of the content of history is necessary. How can this be quickly and painlessly assessed by the busy classroom teacher? As we have emphasised previously, look at the ways this is already being done in your school as the starting point for any staff discussion. The method used by one or other of the teachers may be appropriate for the whole staff to adopt after discussion and reflection in the context of their particular age groups. However, there are some other ways mentioned here in the event of your wishing to encourage the staff to be alert to different ways of assessment. One method that works fairly comfortably in the classroom environment is the True/False/Maybe test. This is equally useful at both Key Stage 1 and Key Stage 2. As subject manager, it may be helpful for you to try this out with your class and then report on its effectiveness and time efficiency to your colleagues.

The basis of the assessment would be a list of questions based on the area of knowledge that had been identified on the medium term plan as a learning objective. For example, in a Key Stage 1 medium term plan, the year group may be studying the lives of their grandparents. A simple assessment would be based on the content studied by the class, and involve questions along the lines of 'Would your grandparents have had a video recorder?' Next to the question would be the words — True, False and Maybe. The children would simply circle the answer required. If literacy is a problem, then it is equally possible to record the test in advance and allow children who need to have alternative arrangements to pencil and paper tests to listen to the taped questions and tell the teacher their answers.

To make the assessment a worthwhile one, it would be necessary to have identified which area of factual knowledge the year group would be focusing on, within the medium term plan. One deputy headteacher we spoke to, Gill Holmes, also offered another idea that is very worthy of consideration. She suggested that a suitable assessment of children's factual knowledge would involve presenting children with a source, perhaps a passage of writing concerning the period being studied. The aim of the assessment would be, again, to focus on a learning objective concerning the acquisition of factual knowledge. For example, a section of text on the religion of the Ancient Egyptians could be presented. The children would then either be given, or read, a series of questions, or even just one question. This question could simply be based on factual knowledge that has been taught to the children, such as 'What is the name of the Egyptian sun god?' The children then have to study the text and underline the name of the god they think is the sun god. For multiple questions, the children can underline in different colours. Again, the task may need to be differentiated to take into account any language difficulties that children may have, so simply put less information on the page. The questions that can be asked can become quite complex and extremely testing — asking children to find the evidence that supports a certain comment, such as — The Egyptians believed in an afterlife — and underlining it is a way of showing progression from simple fact-finding to the manipulation and understanding of, potentially, a range of different sources dealing with the same time period. Both the True/False/Maybe test and the underlining test can be done quickly in the everyday classroom context. It is equally important to find quick and effective ways of assessing children's acquisition of the skills of the historian and it is to these that we now turn our attention.

The key word when implementing assessments is 'minimal'. The whole process needs to take as little time as possible, provide as little disruption as possible, while maximising the information received. It may sound like a step back to the Dark Ages, but the best way to do this is a tick sheet. Before panic sets in, let us clarify our meaning. As we have mentioned in Part 2 of this book, when teachers are preparing their medium term planning for history, it is vital that they include some learning objectives. These learning objectives could be from a 'pool' that must be covered by the year group. For example, one school has a progression of learning in the skill of chronology that builds year on year, from sequencing events to using a number of dates and terms relevant to the passing of time. In Year 3, when the children study Egypt, the terms 'ancient' and 'BC' are introduced. This builds on earlier work in the school, where children are introduced to the terms 'modern' and 'AD'. This is a specific learning objective for the Ancient Egyptians topic, and the teacher is aware of this through the schemes of work, which we will discuss in Part 4. Therefore, in the medium term planning, it will be mentioned that the children are expected to be able to use the terms 'ancient' and 'BC' in the context of their history work. This is hardly a difficult thing to assess. For example, if a child uses the term 'ancient' within a piece of structured history writing, they have achieved the learning objective. The teacher will have a sheet of paper somewhere with the learning objectives written down next to a class list, and they will tick the child's name off for that learning objective and continue with the next target, perhaps, something along the lines of 'using pictures to find out about the daily life of ancient Egyptians'.

In this way, teachers are able to plan in terms of what the child can already do, and offer the children relevant learning experiences which will aid the child's progress as historians. If a child does not meet the specific learning objective, it is covered again, in the same year group, during work on the Romans in Britain, and the teacher will be able to target the children who have not been able to use the terms 'ancient' and 'BC' correctly in their work.

This enables the school to ensure a progression, not of factual knowledge, but of the skills necessary to obtain factual knowledge. The whole scheme is simple to run, and effective, while fulfilling all the needs of the National Curriculum. Apart from that it is also useful. One of your prime concerns as subject manager is that teachers plan their history in an informed manner, to ensure that children receive quality learning experiences. With this assessment system in place, that is exactly what is happening. There are clear objectives, clear guidelines from the policy and schemes of work, and clear use of assessment to inform planning and guide teaching.

It is important, therefore, when constructing the learning objectives to ensure that progression exists from year to year in the skills that you are aiming to assess. There is a definite need for a 'spiralling skills system' to be in place, where each skill is touched upon within as many study units as possible, and the utilisation of the skill requires improvement year on year. For example, looking at interpretations of history, perhaps the key skill, there is a chance to progress, from limited interpretation to fairly complex ones. A Year 3 child studying the Second World War in 'Britain since the 1930s' may be assessed to see if they understand that two different newspapers of the same event (a battle, perhaps) tell different stories because they are reporting from different sides of the battle. This shows a knowledge of interpreting history. A Year 6 child studying the Anglo-Saxons and Vikings may be able to use conflicting sources around the time of the Viking invasions to try and decide who is telling the truth (if anyone), making reference to their knowledge of the period, and other sources they are aware of. This is a much higher order of interpreting history than had been required in Year 3, and therefore shows progression throughout the school's teaching of history.

All of the Key Elements can be sub-divided with a little thought, into a recognisable progression throughout the two Key Stages, and can be fairly comfortably assessed with the minimum of time spent on wasteful paperwork. As the history subject manager, it is your job to ensure that history is taught correctly in your school, and to ensure that all areas of the National Curriculum document are covered. While this is straightforward for the actual content of each study unit, the Key Elements are often neglected. This assessment strategy would satisfy the school's legal requirements in teaching the subject, it would satisfy your need as coordinator to ensure progression in children's learning, and it would satisfy teachers, who would see a positive benefit from implementing the strategy in terms of assisting the accuracy of their planning. Another knock-on benefit comes when reports have to be written, when this assessment strategy will save considerable time and energy for your colleagues.

Another method of recording which is becoming widely used in schools is the 'highlight' method using a cut and paste method of 'parcelling' up the level descriptions. This, again, ties in with the need for learning objectives to be at the forefront of planning. If the agreed aim of the primary school is to follow the expected levels of progression through the National Curriculum, that is, children to be working at Level 2 at the end of Year 2, and at Level 4 at the end of Year 6, then we can use the following example as a means to demonstrate the 'highlight' method.

A Year 2 class has been studying the everyday lives of people in the recent past, using grandparents and parents as a resource, looking at items such as clothing. An identified learning objective is that children show a developing sense of chronology. The assessment used is for children to place items of clothing, or photographs of people in distinctive clothing along a time-line. This fits with the Level Description for Level 2, which states that children show their developing sense of chronology by ordering events and objects. The teacher would fully expect the majority of the class to achieve this particular section of the Level Description. As a result, this sentence is 'highlighted' and it is assumed that all the children have been assessed as being capable of demonstrating this particular skill. Any that achieve above or below this level, that is, Level 1 or Level 3, are noted. This keeps record-keeping down to an absolute minimum — a sheet of paper with a list of children who have either exceeded or not managed to achieve the stated learning objectives and a photocopy of the level descriptions page from the National Curriculum with the performance of the bulk of the children highlighted in the appropriate level.

This method has benefits, especially concerning the amount of time such records would require to be updated and maintained. They also provide an at-a-glance record of the achievement of the majority of the class, so providing the next teacher with the information necessary to plan the next step. Those children who have not managed to achieve the learning objective for the particular skill, in the case of our example, chronology, can progress, and the teacher can allow for the differences of a child working at Level 3. The consistency that is required to make the assessments worthwhile will come from you witnessing and discussing the work of children within a classroom context.

Self assessment by the child

One area of assessment that is sometimes overlooked is the use of self-assessment — where children assess themselves and how they think they have performed in the work. Some schools became embroiled in self-assessments in the early 1990s with the children expected to write huge chunks about their work and, as a result, the whole process became unmanageable.

The best self-assessment we have seen has been extremely simple and equally effective. The simplest of these methods involved the children in drawing smiley faces at the bottom of their work if they thought they had carried it out well, and an unhappy face if they found the work difficult. Those children who are not sure could draw a straight face. The whole process takes seconds and can provide a teacher with invaluable understanding how the child has approached the work.

Another effective method involves 'Thinking Books' where the child keeps a diary of the things they have learned in school. The danger with these books is that they can become simply a catalogue of what was done during the day or week. The teacher needs to focus the children on what they now know that they did not know before. The key to this method is to keep emphasising the learning objectives you have in mind to the children so that they can judge whether they have managed to achieve them, achieved them in part or missed them totally.

Class audit

Children's knowledge of the content of history is necessary. How can the teacher quickly and painlessly assess this? The tick list has a place for looking at the balance of children's historical experiences in a formative way. Below is a very comprehensive and useful list we have seen produced by an LEA. It is useful at the planning stage of a study unit so that teachers can be encouraged to offer a reasonable range of activities with which to explore history. It is also useful as an audit at the end of a study unit to see how far the original aims were achieved. Older children could fill in this audit themselves and thus be made aware of the variety of experiences history learning can offer them. As subject manager, you would be working to build up this audit sheet gradually, over time, from the practice already going on in school. You could work to extend the school's original list into this comprehensive one through personal example, INSET and provision of appropriate resources.

History

KEY STAGE — AUDIT SHEET: PUPILS' LEARNING EXPERIENCES										
TOPIC/UNIT OF WORK **PUPILS' LEARNING EXPERIENCES**										**ACTIVITIES THAT ARE UNDER-USED**
Oral presentation										
Discussion in pairs/groups/class										
Discussion with teacher										
Role-play/drama/games										
Problem-solving										
Self-assessment										
Visual presentation — posters/charts/pictures										
Written presentation										
Analysis and evaluation										
Community involvement										
Local dimension										
Use of artefacts										
Practical classroom activity										
Use of common words/terms										
Site visits/museums, etc.										
Use of dates and chronology to develop a sense of time										
Selection and organisation of historical information/data										
Use of historical documents and printed sources										
Extended narratives										
Outside speakers										
Information Technology										
Video recording/television programmes										
Radio programmes										
Tape recording										
Use of photographs/pictures										
Film strips/slides										
Other literature										
Investigation/research										
Surveys/research										
Textbooks										
Reference books										
Use of oral accounts										
Use of music/drama										
Links with other subjects										

FIG 6.1
Audit sheet

History
A Key Stage 2 planning document using the Programme of Study

Pupils should be taught about important episodes and developments in Britain's past, from Roman to Modern Times, about ancient civilisations and the history of other parts of the world. They should be helped to develop a chronological framework by making links across the different study units. They should have opportunities to investigate local history and to learn about the past from a range of sources of information.

PUPILS SHOULD BE TAUGHT:			YEAR						YEAR					
	TOPICS													
	STUDY UNITS													
Key Elements	Chronology	To place events, people and changes in the periods studied within a chronological framework												
		To use dates/terms relating to the passing of time and terms that define different periods												
	Range and depth of historical knowledge and understanding	About characteristic features of particular periods and societies, including ideas, beliefs and attitudes of people in the past; ■ experiences of men and women ■ social, cultural, religious, ethnic diversity												
		To describe and identify reasons for and results of historical events, situations and changes in the periods studied												
		To describe and make links between the main events, situations and changes both within and across the periods												
	Interpretation	To identify and give reasons for different ways in which the past is represented and interpreted												
	Historical enquiry	How to find out about aspects of the periods studied from a range of sources of information												
		To ask and answer questions and to select and record relevant information												
	Organisation and communication	To recall, select and organise historical information including dates and terms												
		The terms necessary to describe the period and topics studied												
		To communicate their knowledge and understanding in a variety of ways, including structured narratives and descriptions												

© Falmer Press Ltd.

FIG 6.1
Cont'd

History
A Key Stage 2 planning document using the Programme of Study

PUPILS SHOULD BE TAUGHT:			YEAR							YEAR						
		TOPICS														
Study Unit 3b Britain since 1930	Changes in technology and transport	in greater depth about:														
		changes in industry and transport, including the impact of new technologies														
	Britons at war	the impact of the Second World War on the people of Britain														
	The lives of people	at home														
		at work														
		at leisure														
Study Unit 4 Ancient Greece	The Ancient Greeks	Athens and Sparta														
		arts and architecture														
		myths and legends of Greek gods and goddesses, heroes and heroines														
		relations with other people														
	The legacy of Greece	influence on the modern world														
Study Unit 5 Local history	EITHER	an aspect of the local community over a long period of time, i.e.:														
	OR	an aspect of the local community during a short period of time or the local community's involvement in a particular event, i.e.:														
	OR	an aspect of the local community that illustrates developments taught in the study unit, i.e.:														
Study Unit 6 A past non-European society		everyday lives														
		the use of archaeology in finding out about the people and society														

© Falmer Press Ltd.

FIG 6.1
Cont'd

Chapter 9   Responding to children's work and report writing

According to a DFEE circular from March 1996, all pupil reports should include 'brief particulars' of a pupil's progress in subjects that should take the form of a short commentary on the pupil's progress in the subject. The circular states that strengths and particular achievements should be highlighted, together with any particular weaknesses, possibly expressed as targets for development. In other words, the old favourite, that little Billy enjoyed looking at the Tudors, is no longer anywhere near sufficient. OFSTED support this move towards more informative report writing, and have actively sought it out during inspections, making significant mentions depending on a school's effectiveness in reporting properly. This leads to a large problem for some schools, who do not have any assessment procedures in place for foundation subjects. How on earth can a teacher remember the achievements of one of their class in a topic finished in October? One way is to look back through each child's book, but this is exceptionally time consuming. A better alternative would be a brief look at the assessment sheet outlined above, and an accurate report of each child's abilities in the Key Elements. For example, going back to the Year 3 child who has used the terms 'ancient' and 'BC' correctly, the teacher would be able to write that the child is able to use an increasing range of dates and terms relating to the passing of time. If the child did not use the terms correctly, then this could be an area of development, that the child must work on, so the teacher could write something like, 'the child needs to work hard at developing an understanding of terms

used to show the passing of time, such as ancient and BC'.
In this way, your assessment procedure informs not only the
teacher, but the parents as well, and fulfils all the requirements
of the DFEE circular, and OFSTED. The best examples of
reports written have the Key Elements in mind, and are written
in a way that is parent friendly, in that the comments include
reference to the work that has actually been done in class. It
is important to remember that while as teachers we have
requirements to fulfil, such as the DFEE circular, we must also
not lose sight of who reports are for. Parents will not glean
anything useful from a list of Key Elements achieved, without
any context. They will, however, find the skills that must be
reported useful when placed in the context of the work
actually being done in school as their children may well have
talked about the topic at home.

Marking children's work

As we have discussed throughout this book, it is necessary
to consider carefully what history is as a subject, and as a
discipline. This must guide the marking of children's work in
the subject. There are plenty of pitfalls to marking history, but
you must consider what it is that you are marking. All teachers
form opinions of their children's ability through the work that
they mark, and history is no different. However, is it really
history that you are marking? You need to consider carefully
whether or not you are marking a piece of work from a
historical standpoint, or for the ability of the child to write
English. Historical skill is considerably different to the skills
required in English, and as such, spelling and punctuation are
not the key areas of your concern. Your main concern when
marking history is the history, nothing else. Has the child
understood what they are studying, have they gained an
insight into a different time period, and a different way of life?
Does the child utilise historical skills, and question the source
material? Has the child enquired and questioned, or merely
repeated what the teacher or book has already told them? In
a subject where enquiry is the absolute key to the discipline,
why accept a passage of work that fails in this, simply because
it is neatly written and contains no spelling errors? As we
have discussed in Part 2, what you should be providing for
the children in the school is a chance to find out, investigate

FIG 7.1

A Viking Life.

A dreary wooden hut,
A chilly, dark night.
The pigs in the mud,
Some dogs in a fight.

There was an old lady telling stories,
People thought she was a witch.
Some little brown puppy with an old Collie bitch

Children laying down to sleep,
In front of the fire,
In the middle of the night, all cold dark and dire.
People yawning, people streching.
Getting ready to go to sleep,
Ready for another day.

and question. They should not believe everything they read, so why should they simply copy out chunks of a textbook?

As subject manager, you will know the value of staff discussion on children's history work to encourage a common view of what history learning is and how it is portrayed. Children's written work is a useful way for this to be practised with the staff, but always emphasise that oral and dramatic history work also occur, but are less amenable to whole staff discussion (unless taped or videoed). Staff discussion should be continually brought around to the history content and learning which seems to be displayed in written work rather than the English in which it is housed. Figures 7.1–7.4b are examples for your consideration which may

FIG 7.2

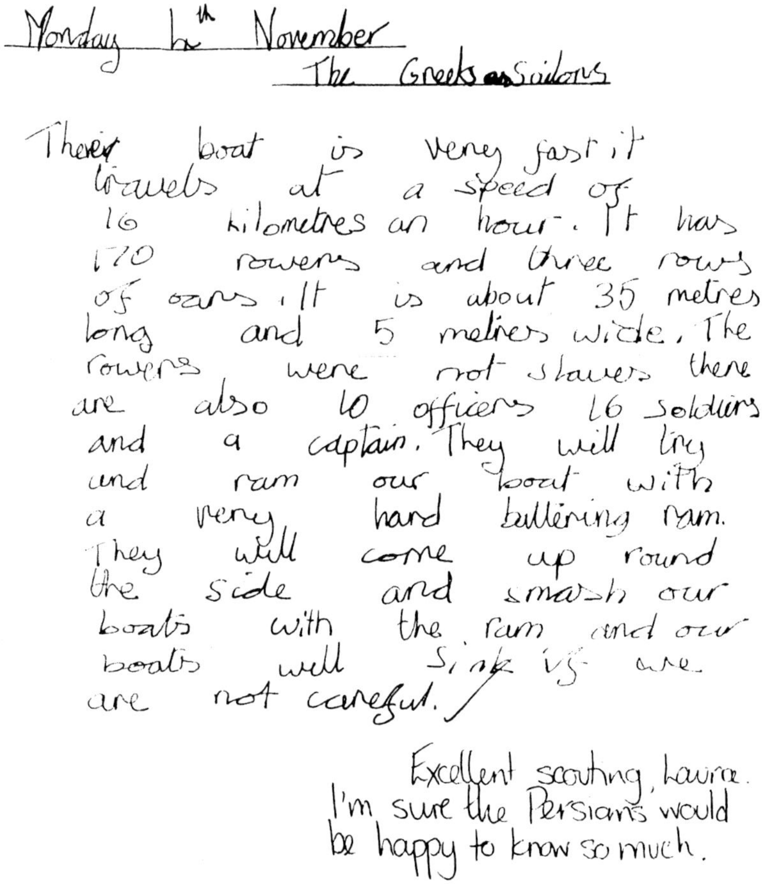

Monday 6th November
The Greeks as Sailors

Their boat is very fast it travels at a speed of 16 kilometres an hour. It has 170 rowers and three rows of oars. It is about 35 metres long and 5 metres wide. The rowers were not slaves there are also 10 officers 16 soldiers and a captain. They will try and ram our boat with a very hard battering ram. They will come up round the side and smash our boats with the ram and our boats will sink if we are are not careful.

Excellent scouting, Laura. I'm sure the Persians would be happy to know so much.

help you in your INSET work (using your children's work of course).

Figure 7.1 was written by a Year 5 pupil as part of the follow up work to a visit to Jorvik, the Viking settlement at York. What historical knowledge, skills and concepts are displayed in this writing? It is empathetic. It also displays knowledge of the period — children lying down to sleep in front of the fire; the term 'hut' is used: animals are named which are used by the Viking people. It touches on the experiences of women and children. Looking at the Key Elements, it is possible to pull out the history in the writing and analyse it.

Figure 7.2 was stimulated by the teacher giving the children different sources on Greek triremes which they then used to write a spy's report to the Persians before the battle of Salamis (Year 4). This pupil's work indicates a high level of understanding of what the Persians would wish to know (empathy). She has analysed the source material and picked

FIG 7.3

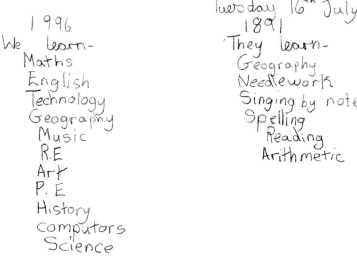

1996
We learn-
Maths
English
Technology
Geography
Music
R.E
Art
P. E
History
computers
Science

Tuesday 16th July
1891
They learn-
Geography
Needlework
Singing by note
Spelling
Reading
Arithmetic

We learn computers they do not have them, they werent invention They have needlework because in 1891 the girls only did needlework for a living. They didn't know about History. They didn't have technology because there were no tools.

out the relevant information (selected and organised historical information including terms). She has communicated the knowledge and understanding through a concise report.

This Year 3 child's lists of similarities and differences (Figure 7.3) between schools in 1996 and 1891 indicates a range and depth of historical knowledge and understanding. An original inspector's report was used to get the information about 1891. It is a piece which should encourage teacher discussion largely because of the opinions the child appends to the lists. In her view, the jobs that girls did in 1891 were restricted to needlework. Technology did not exist because there were no tools — this sentence next to one which indicates that technology was alive and well in 1981 is an insight into the view that the child has of technology. Formative assessment would indicate that work needs to be done to explore the lives of girls in 1891 as well as to discuss technology through history (from the first tools).

FIG 7.4a

Detail from Greek pot see
museum table

Hecles
in Greek
pot

A Museum table

This is a Greek Plate found in
Athens temple it was made in 500BC
it was found in June 1986.
It has a lot of information
on it like they played music
they had olive trees they had
olives they had stone beds
with mattresses on they had
cousonis hodeses mesenger
they had goods they had
clothes and cloth it was made in
Greac it was hand made.

Excellent
detail.

FIG 7.4b

Artefacts.

The object I drew was an old fashioned camera. It's purpose is to take photographs of people and objects. First you had to open the camera up then put the film in and wind it up. Then push the camera down and look through the hole and take a picture.

The camera was just the same size as they are now. Where you look out of the underneath that is like a springy material. Behind that is like a board where you fold it over

Figures 7.4a and 7.4b show how artefacts can be used in different ways. The museum label produced by a Year 4 child indicates a high level of observation was used to write a label which gave an insight of what life may have been like in 500

BC in Ancient Greece. The camera label by a Year 6 child was carefully descriptive of the object but also offered views of the similarity and difference of cameras then and now.

It will be useful when looking at children's work for its historical quality to have a copy of the Key Elements and the level descriptions so that these can be referred to at all times when you or staff offer comments. In this way, the English that the work is housed in will not mask the history that is the focus of the discussion.

Part five Resources for learning

Chapter 10
Gaining, maintaining and using
resources

The teacher is the most important resource in the classroom. However, the quality of history teaching will be expedited or hampered, even in the most gifted teacher's class, by the availability and appropriateness of the resources the school has collected to support the teaching and learning of National Curriculum history. This section addresses the key role of the history subject manager in gaining, maintaining and using sources for history.

Gaining, maintaining and using resources

The National Curriculum has emphasised the process side of history and demands that children be allowed to learn about the past from a wide range of historical sources, including:

 artefacts, pictures and photographs, music, adults talking about their past, documents and printed sources, buildings and sites and computer based material.

Two problems immediately spring to mind.

Where do you get resources from?

If you remember that one of your main purposes in teaching history to children is to give them a sense of personal identity then you will look for sources within the community that the school serves. Artefacts — the correct term for objects looked at historically — are plentiful in every house and garden. Think of the change there has been in irons over the last fifteen years (even if you cannot get any older than that). Children will bring in pieces of clothing, books and various household utensils which can be handled in a historical way to discuss change and continuity, causation and time. Similarly, pictures and photographs are readily available to be used. A letter requesting artefacts from home for a particular topic will result in pupils bringing in a bewildering array of objects. Some schools still have access to loan collections which can be utilised when appropriate. The older members of the community are treasure troves of memories and opinions and welcome being interviewed about any of their experiences. The use of local experts such as archaeologists, local archivists and museum curators broadens children's historical diet. Local crafts people and musicians, retired policemen, teachers, carpenters etc., add to the variety of historical sources that can be effectively tapped within communities. The local built environment is near at hand, familiar yet interesting to budding historians. Written sources do not have to be marriage or birth certificates. They can be local newspaper accounts of famous local events or sporting stories, they can be postcards and letters from different periods, or the school log, old advertisements, recipe books or catalogues.

As subject manager, you have a role in the collection of resources. However, it is not up to you to do all the running around to gather them up. Rather it is to help support and direct your colleagues' energies towards fruitful areas of artefacts and such like. Their enthusiasm and confidence in teaching history as process will grow as they begin to make personal contributions to the resource centre.

How do you make the best use of resources?

In a sense, of course, you will have had specific aids in mind to focus your collections so you and the staff will be committed to teaching and assessing history already, through first hand experiences using primary or secondary sources wherever possible. Having said that, there is still a good deal of INSET to be done to ensure that teachers use the resources in a historically accurate way to develop children's historical understanding. Too often, the activity can end up as a useful oral language session or an inspiring art and design experience rather than a session which extends children's historical concepts. To keep a check on how resources are used and the effectiveness of this, it helps to have clarified, through staff meetings, the purpose of any materials introduced into the classroom for the teaching and learning of history. Below we have listed the key types of materials with references for you to follow up on their uses in the classroom. It is essential that the process of coming to one's own understandings about the merits or demerits of particular resources is discussed with the staff rather than they be given a list and told to get on with it.

Resources and references

Below is a brief and indicative section on resources with what we consider to be key publications where appropriate. Each section can be expanded into a section in your school history resource file.

A great deal of help can be obtained from the Historical Association on many aspects of history. Write to:

The Historical Association,
59a Kennington Park Road,
London, SE11 4JH.
(0171) 735 3901.

I Artefacts

What are artefacts?

Artefacts are objects made by people. They can be as small as a bead or as large as a building. Looking at them in a critical, evaluative way can be useful in revealing many aspects of the past to children and can also lead to cross curricular links being naturally and effectively made.

Why use artefacts?

It is also important to use objects to develop an understanding of the lives of people who provide no permanent written record about themselves. These groups are by no means insignificant. The urban poor are such a case. Their own written record of their lives is extremely sparse, levels of literacy made this inevitable. Through an exploration of their dwellings and possessions — as well as their workplaces — a picture can be built of their lives. Babies leave no written record, but through their clothes, toys and other equipment we can gain insight into their experiences. People who were non-literate, such as the Celts, left no written record of themselves — anything written about them was done by another people who had their own views on what the Celts were like. To hear the voice of the Celt you will need to examine their artefacts that have survived. This is an enormously exciting task for historians who normally love to do this. Getting teachers and children to view artefacts in this way is an important aspect of your job.

The importance of using objects throughout the study units must be stressed for the reasons already mentioned. It is also important to stress that all children, whatever the levels of their literacy skills, can become historians when confronted with an object.

Where can we obtain artefacts?

One practical problem immediately springs to mind. Where will we get artefacts for the Vikings, Romans, Anglo-Saxons, Ancient Greeks or Tudors — even if we can manage to get some for other study units? There may well be a loan service available in your area from local museums and should be used, but the likelihood of the museum being willing or able to loan artefacts to service all units is slim. It is even more unlikely that the curator would be willing to loan fragile and irreplaceable objects from the past for use with primary children. You can and should ensure teachers take their classes to view these things as housed in the museum.

How to handle artefacts

The handling of objects also needs to be done by teachers and children on a regular basis. One way to achieve this is by the judicious use of authentic reproductions. These fakes allow us to see and feel what a whole Roman bowl, for example, would be like. Without these, children would have had the chance of handling broken pottery pieces and then looking at pictures of what a complete bowl was like. It is difficult for young children to make sense of fragments or to get any real sense of how the bowl might have been used or what it looked like. The idea of using reproductions needs to be thoroughly discussed by the staff so that a consensus of how to introduce them to the children is agreed. You will be careful to stress the uses of original and contemporary materials whenever possible, but the extra opportunities offered by using replicas to illuminate the past for the children needs to be spelled out alongside the need to tell children which sources are reproductions and why you need to use them.

Two addresses of firms which specialise in replicas are

History in Evidence,
Unit 4, Holmewood Fields Business Park,
Park Road,
Holmewood,
Chesterfield,
S42 5UY.

and

Milestone Pottery,
Unit 234F,
Redwither Industrial Estate,
Wrexham,
Clwyd,
LL13 9UH

An excellent book for teachers to use as a basis for their planning in using artefacts with their children is detailed below.

DURBIN, G., MORRIS, S. and WILKINSON, S. (1990) *A Teacher's Guide to Learning from Objects*, English Heritage.

2 Portraits and pictures

You will support and enhance children's history learning through the wide use of visual evidence by teachers who are aware of its power and limitation.

First, the use of visual material as sources of evidence about the past is obligatory. The National Curriculum Programme of Study spells this out. Second, pictures of all types have an immediate impact on children, through them children can become engaged at first hand in studying the past by using them as historical sources. Portraits provide excellent opportunities to develop children's ability to acquire evidence from historical sources and form judgments about their reliability and value.

Picture collections

In order for the children to have as wide an experience as possible of working with this evidence base, it is useful for you to encourage the staff to make collections which cover the various types of materials on which pictures are found. The word picture covers a wide range of historical sources and can include:

- paintings
- sketches
- cartoons
- drawings
- engravings
- tapestries
- pictures on pottery
- pictures on stamps
- statues
- carvings
- pictures on song sheets
- advertisements
- photographs
- film
- video
- portraits

The central history resource section in your school should have a flavour of as many of these items as possible.

Using pictures

You will have discussed the ways to handle pictorial evidence with the staff and come to a consensus of the need to develop the skill of picture reading in the children. This requires a commitment to teach this and to give structured practice in it.

Above all, the children need to be taught to ask questions of the pictures. It is useful here to add a few words as an aide memoire for the teachers about this.

Investigating a picture

There are various **levels of questioning** which need to be practised:

The first is to pose questions which involve looking closely at a picture to pick out observational detail such as the number and gender of the people. Questions about their clothing, the background and so on encourage children to really look at a picture. The inferential level of questioning to be used on a picture would ask such things as: Why are they doing that?; or What sort of mood is she in? Here we are in the realm of opinion which may or may not be supported by other sources. The weight that is given to the suppositions will depend on the production of supplementary evidence. The use of opinion expressed in textbooks should not be valued too highly if there is no reference to source material on which it is based. This may sound harsh but **history is largely opinion and this needs to be emphasised to the children**.

Resources to further teachers' effective use of pictures include:
MORRIS, S.A. *Teachers' Guide to Using Portraits*, English Heritage, 1990.
DEVELOPMENT EDUCATION CENTRE (1989) *Get the Picture! Developing Visual Literacy in the Infant Classroom*, Birmingham DEC.

In addition, several companies produce videos showing past events, for example, Parkfield Pathe News with videos for each year from 1931 to 1969.

Useful for INSET purposes, English Heritage produce a slide pack 'Using Portraits' which takes you through twelve slides with careful notes so that your observation skills are enhanced. This can be used during INSET activities on handling evidence.

3 Stories and narrative

As history subject manager, you will be emphasising the rationale behind the centrality of story in history teaching. The story form is a cultural universal — everyone everywhere enjoys stories. No one should underestimate the power of the well-told tale. Stories and narrative are essential to history teaching. There is an important and central place in history for 'good stories, well told', for narrative offered by the teacher and by the pupils — and for pupils to be taught to listen carefully and critically.

Why use narrative to teach history?

There are several sound, educational reasons for using story to teach history:

> Stories are the natural way in which sequence, causation and change can be explored. For KS1 especially, but not exclusively, they can provide a vehicle for developing language, a chronological sense, environmental understanding and for stimulating a range of work in art, technology, music drama etc.

We need to bear in mind Margaret Meek's view: tales read with pleasure singly or shared are remembered for a lifetime; the contents of a textbook have a less assured survival. In other words, if history is to be considered exciting and pleasurable, the use of stories will be part of all teachers' resource material.

The history narrative collection

There will be a need to build up a stock of stories to support the study units. The stories should be told from a variety of perspectives and be used as evidence bases for exploration by the children. It is obligatory that the repertoire of historical stories you develop in your school should be drawn from a variety of **cultures** and periods of **time**:

1   well-known myths and legends; stories about the past read or told at story-time;
2   suitable extracts from reminiscences, memoirs and diaries; versions of real historical events told as fiction;
3   stories related to anniversaries as they occur;
4   stories and historical writing which relate to other sources studied by the pupils.

Useful publications

HMI (1985) *History in the Primary and Secondary Years*, DES.

HMI (1989) *Aspects of Primary Education. The Teaching and Learning of History and Geography*, DES.

COX, K. and HUGHES, P. *Early Years History: An Approach Through Story*, Liverpool Institute of Higher Education, Stand Park Road, Liverpool, L16 9JD.

FARMER, A. 'Story-telling in history', *Teaching History*, January, 1990.

LITTLE, V. and JOHN, T. (1988) 'Historical fiction in the classroom', *Teaching of History*, Series No.59, The Historical Association.

Sets of books are also available from:

MADELINE LINDLEY, *Early Years History: An Approach Through Story*, 79 Acorn Centre, Barry Street, Oldham, OL1 3NE.

Stories for Time book box from
Badger Publishing Limited,
Unit One, Parsons Green Estate,
Boulton Road,
Stevenage, Herts, SG1 4QG.

WILSON, V. and WOODHOUSE, J. (1990) *History Through Drama: A Teachers' Guide*, The Historical Association.

4 Oral history

Why oral history?

Oral history has a role in all primary schools. It is an important source of evidence for the Key Stage 1 history curriculum as well as the Local History Unit and the Britain since the 1930's study unit. It can be used as a way of looking at the experiences of groups that might otherwise be lost in recorded history — the urban and rural poor women who worked outside and inside the home during this century depending on the labour needs of the country at the time.

Oral history collection

Oral history collection by children encourages them to develop personal and practical skills which are of use to them long after the history topic they were engaged in ends. As subject manager, you can encourage staff to give children the direct experience of collecting data from people by pointing out the benefits. They will be collecting source material at first hand. Children learn the valuable skills of developing self-confidence, taking responsibility for their own time management as well as for the series of questions they have planned to ask the source (perhaps an eighty-five year old who is hearing impaired). In addition, they will be introduced to the practicalities of working a tape recorder or video camera. Finally, and most importantly, they will learn the skills of transcribing tapes and the way that historians and others are able to manipulate evidence in order to offer a particular slant on things.

The main national centre for oral history is the National Sound Archive which is part of the British Library which has produced oral history packs for use in schools. A great deal of useful work has also been done at the local level. Teachers can contact the archive and be referred to their local project, library, county record office, museum or sound archive of which the NSA holds all the relevant details. The archive offers teachers an oral history reference library and listening facilities and can make copies (at a price) of tapes in its collection.

COCKROFT, J. (1986) *In My Time*, Collins Educational.
PURKIS, S. (1987) *Thanks for the Memory*, Collins Educational.
REDFERN, A. (1995) *Oral History in Schools*, Oral History
    Society.

The National Sound Archive,
29, Exhibition Road,
London,
SW7 2AS.

5 Buildings and historical sites

For further information on this primary source see the English Heritage series of videos and accompanying booklets for various historic sites. In addition, they produce a series of videos which show how a historian needs to be like a detective in looking for clues and evidence in order to reach conclusions about buildings and objects. These can be fruitfully discussed in staff development time. Information for these and all English Heritage material can be obtained from:

English Heritage Education Service,
Key Sign House,
429, Oxford Street,
London. WAR 2HD
(0171) 973 3442/3.

Information on sites of historical interest also available from:

The National Trust Education Manager,
36 Queen Anne's Gate,
London, SW1H 9AS. (0171) 222 9251.

The Education Officer,
Council for British Archaeology,
The King's Manor,
York.
YO1 2EP.
(01904) 433 925.

Museums
Group for Education in Museums,
c/o Chatham Historic Dockyard Trust,
Chatham, Kent.
ME4 4TE.

An organisation for all concerned with the educational use of museums, galleries and sites.

The Museum Association,
42 Clerkenwell Close,
London,
(0171) 608 2933.

This association publishes the *Museum Yearbook*, which lists all British museums and galleries and publishes the monthly 'Museums' Journal'.

Local history
British Association for Local History,
Ashwell Education Services,
Merchant Taylors Centre,
Ashwell,
Baldock,
Herts.
SG7 5LY.

6 Written sources

Collecting written sources

There is a rich variety of documentary material available such as school log books, census returns, parish records, letters, inventories and government reports, marriage and birth certificates and wills. In addition, newspapers, directories, advertisements, posters and other printed matter provide useful material on which to work.

Original documentation will probably be precious and available only to look at carefully and not to work from. Photocopies of these are a good substitute for they provide children with a chance to study the layout, language and writing of the original without fear of damage. You should collect as wide a variety of these materials as possible but it is essential to catalogue them and to ensure that staff know their whereabouts and that they have decided how best they may be used. Written sources will need to be subjected to careful scrutiny so that bias can be a consideration in the children's understanding of the past as presented by them.

Ways to use written sources

It will help staff to have had a discussion on the usefulness of asking historian's questions of the material.

Is there more than one point of view expressed in the material?
From whose point of view is the material written?
Are other sources referred to, to support the point of view?
Are they available in full to be explored afresh?

One aspect of documentary evidence needs exploring with the staff. A piece of writing from Victorian times will be difficult for children to decipher. Should this be translated into present day script? The answer depends on what you want the children to get from it.

Essentially, the medium is as important as the message so should not be tampered with lightly. The very act of carefully looking at and deciphering text is an important and necessary skill for all historians and one children should be inducted into as soon as possible.

Useful sources of written materials

COCKROFT, J. (1986) *The Census*, Collins Educational.
DEVELOPMENT EDUCATION CENTRE (1991) *New Journeys:
Teaching about other places*, Birmingham DEC.
MCFARLANE, C. (1986) *Hidden Messages? Activities for
Exploring Bias*, Birmingham, DEC.

One pack of documents which makes the past accessible to children has been produced by:

Charlotte Mason College and Cumbria Archive Service *Could Do Better. Children at School 1870–1925.*

BLYTH, J. and HUGHES, P. (1997) *Using Written Sources in Primary History*, London, Hodder and Stoughton.

This book is a practical guide to the use of written sources in primary school. There are over fifty original British sources, ranging from Roman times to the twentieth century, complete with a commentary of teaching suggestions. The sources include extracts from contemporary accounts, charters, diaries, interviews, letters, inventories, school books advertisements, memorials, historical and children's fiction.

7 Living history

Living history involves children in a dramatic reconstruction of an event in the past. It is useful to inform staff of what is available within reasonable travelling distance in terms of 'In Role' days so that these can be planned within a topic rather than become a bolt-on after thought. The costs involved make it essential that there is maximum follow-up, so that the children get the most out of the experience and the governors and parents feel the money has been well spent.

8 Information Technology

Information Technology's first and most significant contribution to the history curriculum lies in the data bases that can be created to deal with the material generated from studies involving the local community such as census returns or school rolls.

The second area where IT can enhance the history curriculum is through the series of computer aided learning programs becoming readily available from publishers. You will need to be discriminating in the choice of programs and choose ones which will fully support effective teaching.

National Council for Educational Technology,
Sir William Lyons Road,
Science Park,
Coventry.
CV4 7EZ.

9 Published history schemes and television programmes

One important piece of information which you need to disseminate to staff regularly until they have absorbed it, is that HMI found that where there was poor primary history practice there was also over-reliance on TV programmes and published schemes. Teachers must come to an understanding that schemes can be useful if used selectively but are not the complete answer to history teaching. There is good material on the market, of course, but there is also a lot that is not suitable for teaching history as effectively as a resource bank built specifically to meet the needs of a particular set of children tackling a particular study unit.

10 Equal opportunities and multicultural education

National Curriculum history requires that children be taught about the cultural and ethnic diversity of past societies and the experiences of men and women. Therefore, each time a study unit is planned these two requirements should be carefully catered for. We have all been exposed to history teaching supported by textbooks which have largely ignored the part played by women and minority ethnic groups in the development of our society. We must be aware of this bias in our own knowledge so that we do not pass it on by default to our children. Your school will no doubt have an equal opportunities and multicultural education set of guidelines. It would seem sensible to use the principles involved in setting up those as a basis for planning your history units. Below are two references we have found useful as a starting point for staff discussions. We have also included an example of a local reference to indicate that there are groups around the country who work at a local level and find local material that would be relevant to you, wherever you are. Bear in mind Thomas Carlyle's observation that 'The history of the world is but the biography of great men' when viewing resources from an equality point of view.

References

COLLICOTT, S. (1991) 'A Woman's Place', *Junior Education*, May.

COLLICOTT, S. (1986) *Connections*, Haringey Local-National-World Links. (Available from Haringey Community Information Service in association with the Multicultural Curriculum Support Group, Central Library, Wood Green, High Road, London, N22.)

MANCHESTER WOMEN'S HISTORY GROUP (1995) *Resources for Women's History in Greater Manchester*, Manchester: National Museum of Labour History Publication.

Concluding remarks

Your commitment to history teaching and learning of quality is vital. Hopefully, you will not be the unwilling conscript who has drawn the short straw of history: you will be the enthusiastic volunteer who will inspire her colleagues through her love of the subject. There seems no better way of developing staff confidence in teaching history than for you to pilot various methods and materials and to share your findings with them, in the first instance, before encouraging them to share their own successes with the rest of the staff. Staff development exercises which involve looking not just at how to use a resource but also how to plan for progression in its use is another way in which you can ensure children get a broadly balanced history curriculum. Ultimately, as we have said, your personal enthusiasm for history will be a crucial factor in the staff's commitment to its place in the primary curriculum.

References

BOYLE, B. (1995) 'Providing a sense of direction in Key Stage 2', in HARRISON, M. (ed.) *Developing a Leadership Role in Key Stage 2 Curriculum*, London: Falmer Press.

CROSS, A. and HARRISON, M. (1994) 'Succesful curriculum change through coordination', in HARRISON, M. (ed.) *Beyond the Core Curriculum*, Plymouth: Northcote House.

DEAN, J. (1987) *Managing the Primary School*, Kent: Croon Helm.

DURBIN, G., MORRIS, S. and WILKINSON, S. (1990) *A Teacher's Guide to Learning from Objects*, London: English Heritage.

EVERARD, K.B. and MORRIS, G. (1985) *Effective School Management*, London: PCP.

HARRISON, M. (ed.) (1995a) *Developing a Leadership Role in the Key Stage 2 Curriculum*, London: Falmer Press.

HARRISON, M. (1995b) 'Developing the skills to become an effective Key Stage 1 subject coordinator', in DAVIES, J. (ed.) *Developing a Leadership Role in Key Stage 1 Curriculum*, London: Falmer Press.

HARRISON, M. and GILL, S. (1992) *Primary School Management*, London: Heinemann.

LLOYD, K. (1994) 'Place and practice in the current state of geography in the primary curriculum', *Primary Geographer*, **17**, p. 3.

Index

ORDER FORM

Post: *Customer Services Department, Falmer Press, Rankine Road, Basingstoke, Hampshire, RG24 8PR*
Tel: *(01256) 813000* **Fax**: *(01256) 479438*
E-mail: *book.orders@tandf.co.uk*

10% DISCOUNT AND FREE P&P FOR SCHOOLS OR INDIVIDUALS ORDERING THE COMPLETE SET - ORDER YOUR SET NOW. WITH CREDIT CARD PAYMENTS, YOU WON'T BE CHARGED TILL DESPATCH.

TITLE	DUE	ISBN	PRICE	QTY
SUBJECT LEADERS' HANDBOOKS SET		**(RRP £207.20)**	**£185.00**	
Coordinating Science	2/98	0 7507 0688 0	£12.95	
Coordinating Design and Technology	2/98	0 7507 0689 9	£12.95	
Coordinating Maths	2/98	0 7507 0687 2	£12.95	
Coordinating Physical Education	2/98	0 7507 0693 7	£12.95	
Coordinating History	2/98	0 7507 0691 0	£12.95	
Coordinating Music	2/98	0 7507 0694 5	£12.95	
Coordinating Geography	2/98	0 7507 0692 9	£12.95	
Coordinating English at Key Stage 1	4/98	0 7507 0685 6	£12.95	
Coordinating English at Key Stage 2	4/98	0 7507 0686 4	£12.95	
Coordinating IT	4/98	0 7507 0690 2	£12.95	
Coordinating Art	4/98	0 7507 0695 3	£12.95	
Coordinating Religious Education	Late 98	0 7507 0613 9	£12.95	
Management Skills for SEN Coordinators	Late 98	0 7507 0697 X	£12.95	
Building a Whole School Assessment Policy	Late 98	0 7507 0698 8	£12.95	
Curriculum Coordinator and OFSTED Inspection	Late 98	0 7507 0699 6	£12.95	
Coordinating Curriculum in Smaller Primary School	Late 98	0 7507 0700 3	£12.95	

Value of Books	
P&P*	
Total	

I wish to pay by:

*Please add p&p
orders up to £25   *10%*
orders from £25 to £50   *5%*
orders over £50   *free*

❑ Cheque *(Pay* Falmer Press*)*
❑ Pro-forma invoice
❑ Credit Card *(Mastercard / Visa / AmEx)*

Card Number _____ *Expiry Date* _____
Signature _____
Name _____ *Title/Position* _____
School _____
Address _____
_____
Postcode _____ *Country* _____
Tel no. _____ *Fax* _____
E-mail _____

❑ If you do not wish to receive further promotional information from the Taylor&Francis Group, please tick box.
All prices are correct at time of going to print but may change without notice

Ref: 1197BFSLAD